Teammate Tuesdays

Volume V

Another Year of Good Teammate Musings

LANCE LOYA

CAGER HAUS PUBLISHING

www.coachloya.com

Design and publishing by Cager Haus.
Cover image by Kutsal Lenger, Dreamstime.com.

For Laken and Lakota…may you always be good teammates.

Contents

v

Acknowledgements

Another year leads to another book! I want to once again offer a special thank you to Wendy Clouner for suggesting that I start a blog. Although I wasn't initially receptive to your suggestion, I am glad I eventually acquiesced. Here we are five years later, and we're still going strong. I also want to express my gratitude to Rachel Loya and Cindy Davis for your continued support and recommendations.

I would also like the thank my Good Teammate Factory clients and the online community members who read blogs, listen to podcasts, like and share social media posts, and offer invaluable feedback and encouragement. You are the fuel that powers the *Be a Good Teammate* movement.

Introduction

Welcome to *Teammate Tuesdays Volume V*! I can't begin to convey how much assembling another book of this nature makes my heart smile. Let me share with you how the *Teammate Tuesdays* book series came to be.

Once upon a time, I set out on a journey to discover an answer to the question: *What does it mean to be a good teammate?* Everybody belongs to some type of team. Maybe it's an actual sports team, or maybe it's the place where you work, the community you live in, the church you attend, or simply your family. Ultimately, the success of any team depends on the capacity of its members to be good teammates. But what specifically does being a "good teammate" entail?

My journey began with the publication of a children's book called *Be a Good Teammate*. The book revolved around the idea that good teammates do three things: care, share, and listen. I wrote that book with the sole intention of conveying some fatherly advice to my daughters, who, at the time, were learning to read.

The publication of *Be a Good Teammate* unexpectedly set into motion a sequence of events that changed the trajectory of my life and led me to the realization that the world needs more good teammates—kind, mindful, unselfish individuals who put the needs of their teams ahead of any individual agendas. This belief transcends sports and applies to all varieties of teams.

The journey eventually brought me to a point where exploring the art of being a good teammate became my life's work. Somewhere along the way, I decided to heed the advice of a trusted friend and share my discoveries—my *musings*—in a weekly blog. I called the blog "Teammate Tuesdays" and posted a new entry every Tuesday morning.

As the blog's following grew, subscribers began reaching out to me about the possibility of making the content available in print form. They wanted to give the blog as a gift to their friends, families, and teams. To accommodate the recurring requests, I turned the entire first year of my blog into a book titled *Teammate Tuesdays: A Year of Good Teammate Musings*.

The book you're presently reading is a compilation of the entire fifth year of my blog. Like the previous volumes, this book will provide you with an abundance of "good teammate" stories, observations, and insights—each intended to make you think about what kind of teammate you are.

It should be noted that this book is written in a more informal, conversational tone—the way blogs typically are.

Each post (chapter) was written as an independent entity. With a few minor exceptions, like the removal of embedded hyperlinks and the addition of appropriate citations, the content has not been altered from how it originally appeared online.

Topics covered in this year's volume include humility, empathy, and maintaining individuality while still being a good teammate. This volume also introduces readers to a variety of different types of teammates, like Elevator Teammates, Armadillo Teammates, Icarus Teammates, and Stay-In-Your-Lane Teammates.

I continue to like the idea of assembling an entire year's worth of posts in a book format. The content is worth sharing in an alternative medium. Not everyone who can benefit from the message reads blogs. Some people still prefer to hold a physical book in their hands. Putting the blog in book form makes it possible to share the message with a broader audience.

A book is also a convenient way to bring up to speed those who may be joining the Good Teammate movement *already in progress*. The format allows you to experience your own journey of discovery, at your own pace. You don't have to wait until next week to find out what topic I am going to cover in my blog. You can read the chapters as fast or slow as you desire. It's like binge reading a blog.

I am often asked two questions: *Why Tuesdays?* and *Why doesn't the first chapter start on January 1?*

We all have seasons to our lives. For some, it's spring, summer, fall, and winter. For those involved in sports, it's preseason, regular season, postseason, and offseason. I wrote my initial blog post at the end of April, coinciding with what was at that time considered to be the start of my offseason—the ideal time to start new endeavors. I have consistently added a new post every week since then, which is why the first chapter doesn't start on January 1.

Why Tuesdays? I am a fan of Mitch Albom's memoir *Tuesday's with Morrie*. In the book, he chronicles the wisdom acquired from his weekly visits with his former sociology professor Morrie Swartz, who is dying from ALS. The name *Teammate Tuesdays* was a tip of the hat of sorts to Albom's book and its touching premise. But that's not the only reason. I also believe that Tuesdays are generally the best days for personal and professional development.

Wednesdays mark the middle of the week. It's *hump day*. You've come to the realization that you better put your nose to the grindstone and get busy or you're going to run out of time.

Thursdays still have some of the same urgency to get your work done as Wednesdays. But by Thursday afternoon, you are starting to set your sights on the weekend.

Fridays are the day to wrap up loose ends and then coast through the rest of the day. It's the end of the traditional work week, so you're reluctant to start any new projects. You may also feel burned out by Friday and not necessarily motivated to engage in anything mentally taxing.

Saturdays are spent catching up on chores, like cutting grass and doing laundry. Saturdays are additionally a day for recreation and seeking fun.

Sundays are family time. You're ready to relax and spend quality time with your friends and family. If you're struggling with your job, you'll probably spend Sunday evening stressing about having to go back to work the next day. Professional development isn't a high priority on Sundays.

Mondays are consumed with playing catch up. You're trying to finish all the work you didn't complete—but should have—last week. You are probably also being bombarded with everything that was delivered over the weekend. You have an endless amount of pressing emails and phone calls to return. By the time Mondays are over, you are exhausted.

Which brings us to Tuesdays. You are tired from playing catch up on Monday and not anxious to put in another intense day of work. You convince yourself that you still have the rest of the week to get your work done. Why start today? Tuesdays are the perfect day to invest in self-improvement.

Sound familiar? If so, then you've come to the right place. Every day is *Tuesday* in this book.

I hope you enjoy my collection of good teammate musings. My wish is for them to inspire you to become a better version of yourself and to equip you with the tools to help others do the same.

Good Teammate Move

/ ˈgu̇d – ˈtēm · māt – müv / **noun.** a kind, generous, selfless act committed by an individual member of a team for the sole purpose of helping his or her team.

The term *good teammate move* appears numerous times throughout this book. The concept was first introduced in the inaugural volume of *Teammate Tuesdays*. While the context surrounding the term generally provides sufficient understanding of its meaning, consider the following: Dancers have moves. They plié, pirouette, and lean-and-dab. The more dance moves they have, the better dancer they are. Basketball players have moves. They spin, crossover, and go behind their backs. The more moves they have, the better player they are. The same rationale applies to good teammates. The more good teammate moves you make, the better teammate you are.

The Humility to Listen
APRIL 27

Listening is an important part of being a good teammate. Teammates who listen facilitate efficiency, increase productivity, and minimize grief. Listening leads to team success, especially when it involves listening to feedback.

This week in 1985, The Coca-Cola Company launched "New Coke," a reformulated version of its signature soft drink. The change in formula came in response to Coke's declining presence in the marketplace. Coke had dominated the soft drink market for decades, owning a whopping sixty percent share by the end of World War II. Aggressive competitor advertising and the emergence of diet soda alternatives saw that number shrink to just over twenty percent by the late 1970s.

Pepsi had been steadily gaining ground on Coke and was starting to outsell Coke in grocery stores. Their popular *Pepsi Challenge* campaign demonstrated that consumers preferred Pepsi's sweeter taste—a fact confirmed by Coke's own internal research. With sales sliding and Coke on the verge of losing the Cola War, Coca-Cola executives made the bold decision to change the soft drink's trusted ninety-nine-year-old formula.

After months of testing and tinkering, Coke unveiled a new, sweeter tasting formula. At first, consumers latched onto the new taste. The launch led to an immediate spike in sales, and New Coke became the water cooler's trendiest topic. Everyone was talking about New Coke. But the hype was short-lived. Within a few weeks, the company began to experience backlash. Stock prices plummeted as tens of thousands of angry calls flooded Coke's corporate hotline. Petitions were formed, protests were staged, and lawsuits were filed demanding a return to the old formula.

New Coke became every comedian's go-to punchline. The backlash surprised Coca-Cola executives. They had conducted nearly 200,000 blind taste tests and the data showed that consumers preferred the taste of New Coke over both Pepsi and Coke's original formula. Most experts believe Coca-Cola's *bold decision* backfired because they underestimated their most loyal customers' emotional attachment to the brand.

On July 11, 1985, a mere seventy-nine days after launching the biggest change in the company's history, Coca-Cola held a press conference to announce the return of its original formula. Networks interrupted regular programming to share the big announcement. Donald Keough, then-president of Coca-Cola, said, "Our boss is the consumer. We want them to know we're really sorry."

People appreciated Coke's response. By the end of 1985, Coca-Cola Classic was outselling both New Coke and Pepsi, and Coke's market share increased more than double that of Pepsi. The launch of New Coke is often viewed as the biggest marketing blunder in corporate history. Business schools use the company's *bold decision* to change its formula as an example of why companies shouldn't try to fix what isn't broken.

While that may be true, the company's equally *bold decision* to listen and respond appropriately to their loyal customers' feedback should also be highlighted. Coca-Cola could have ignored the feedback, held firm, and forged ahead despite the backlash. Instead, they wisely chose to listen to what their customers—their "teammates"—were telling them. They then had the courage to set their egos aside and act on what they had heard.

Listening *is* an important part of being a good teammate. But ultimately, the action that follows listening defines a good teammate. Like the Coca-Cola executives, a good teammate must have the humility to listen to feedback and acknowledge flawed decisions—*and* the courage to take the necessary action to amend those decisions.

As always…Good teammates care. Good teammates share. Good teammates listen. Go be a good teammate.

*Statistics and associated information included above are from Dermott, John S. "All Afizz Over the New Coke" Time, June 24, 1985.

** Donald Keough's quotation is from Christopher, Klein. "Why Coca Cola's 'New Coke' Flopped." March 13, 2020. https://www.history.com/news/why-coca-cola-new-coke-flopped

Chef Jennifer and the Quote du Jour
MAY 4

Finding inspiration in an unexpected place, from an unexpected source, results in a special blessing. I had the good fortune of receiving such a blessing over the weekend.

I was in Tampa for a convention and searching for someplace to eat dinner. An employee at my hotel recommended I check out Big Ray's Fish Camp at the Sail Pavilion.

"It's nothing fancy," he said. "But you're going to love it."

Big Ray's Fish Camp is an open-air restaurant overlooking the marina along Tampa's Riverwalk. It's an ideal place to people-watch, listen to music, enjoy sunsets, and eat good food—*really* good food. *(The blackened grouper sandwich is to die for!)* While all those elements contributed to how much I loved eating at Big Ray's, they aren't what made the experience special.

At Big Ray's, food is ordered from a walk-up window and then delivered to your table in an eco-friendly takeout container. When our party's food arrived, we found inspirational quotes written on each container.

The person responsible for the inspirational quotes was Chef Jennifer Dunlap. I learned she personally writes a positive, encouraging message on every order she prepares. The quote on my container read: *Be fearless in your pursuit of what sets your soul on fire.*

That quote happens to be one of my favorites. The message applies to the art of being a good teammate, as good teammates must be fearless in serving the needs of their team. They should pursue this endeavor with burning passion.

Chef Jennifer is an excellent example of the type of teammate you want on your team—someone who goes above and beyond in their service. Teammates like her tip the scale of success in their teams' favor.

Adding handwritten inspirational quotes to orders isn't in her job description. She's not required to inspire customers in that manner. But she does it anyway, and her extra effort is what made dining at Big Ray's special.

Good teammates recognize the value of doing more than what is expected. They don't allow their contributions to be constrained by the limitations of their job descriptions or by what others deem to be sufficient. To good teammates, going the "extra mile" is standard operating procedure.

Everyone at our table was moved by Chef Jennifer's quotes. What she wrote brought smiles to our faces and warmed our hearts. We came to Big Ray's seeking nourishment for our bodies. We left with nourished bodies *and* nourished spirits.

What was on the outside of the containers nourished us as much as what was on the inside.

All good chefs have a recipe with a coveted secret ingredient. Chef Jennifer's secret ingredient is positivity and she adds it to every dish she serves. If you're ever in the Tampa, Florida area, be sure to stop by Big Ray's Fish Camp. I'll bet Chef Jennifer's secret ingredient and her desire to exceed expectations will inspire you too.

As always…Good teammates care. Good teammates share. Good teammates listen. Go be a good teammate.

Visit https://www.facebook.com/bigraysfishcamp/ to learn more about Big Ray's Fish Camp.

Six Signs You're Not as Good of a Teammate as You Think You Are
MAY 11

Most people think of themselves as being good teammates because they recognize *macro selfishness*—obvious, big-picture selfishness. They grasp that disregarding others' feelings, having self-serving motives, and not sharing the credit are selfish behaviors and signs of being a poor teammate.

But many of those same people disqualify themselves as good teammates because they fail to recognize *micro selfishness*—some of the distinction's more subtle nuances.

Here are six signs you might not be as good of a teammate as you think you are:

1. **You have conditional relationships.** Are your relationships governed by restrictive conditions? *I will help you, if you help me. I will get your back, if you get mine.* If your relationships contain these types of

limitations, you might not be as good of a teammate as you think you are. Good teammates understand that not every relationship is going to be mutually beneficial. Sometimes you are going to be asked to carry more than your share of the load—because doing so is what is best for your team. Good teammates don't resent helping others, even when that help isn't reciprocated.

2. **You're not equally excited about your teammates' success.** How do you react to hearing your teammates' good news? If you're not as excited about your teammates' success as you are about your own success, you might not be as good of a teammate as you think you are. Good teammates embrace the idea that *when one of us wins, we all win.* They are never jealous or envious of another teammate's accolades. They celebrate their teammates' individual victories with the same fervor as they would their own victories.

3. **You complain.** How do you respond to problems? If you choose complaining over confronting, you might not be as good of a teammate as you think you are. Good teammates confront problems; they don't complain about them. Confronting involves action and leads to resolution. Complaining is merely airing your displeasure. Good teammates possess the courage to engage problems and the gumption to remedy them.

4. **You are moody.** Do you have a consistent demeanor? If your mood fluctuates the breadth of the spectrum around the other members of your team, you might not be as good of a teammate as you think you are. Good teammates realize their emotional state influences others. They minimize disruptions by avoiding frequent mood swings. Intentionally regulating their mood to meet their teams' needs creates a harmonious environment, conducive to team growth.

5. **You are stingy with praise.** How well do you convey your appreciation for your teammates? If you are stingy with your compliments, you might not be as good of a teammate as you think you are. Good teammates praise regularly, generously, and openly. They don't withhold their acknowledgement, appreciation, or admiration. When a fellow teammate does something that is praiseworthy, they make sure that action is recognized with timely praise.

6. **You despise being inconvenienced.** What is your response to situations that take you out of your comfort zone? If you balk at being inconvenienced, you might not be as good of a teammate as you think you are. Good teammates are willing to sacrifice their personal comfort for their teams' benefit. Nobody enjoys being inconvenienced, but refusing to assist a teammate in need because the

situation is less than ideal for *you* demonstrates a lack of true commitment to your teams' best interests.

The next time you assess how good of a teammate you are, be sure to not discount the above behaviors. Although they seem small, underestimating their impact can be a big mistake.

As always…Good teammates care. Good teammates share. Good teammates listen. Go be a good teammate.

Rowing with Concertion and Faith
MAY 18

What image comes to mind when you hear the word *teamwork*? Is it an image of a sports team putting their hands together in a huddle? Is it an image of people pulling on the same rope? Is it an image of interlinking gears?

If you search the internet for images of teamwork, many of the top results are photos of rowing teams. I find rowing images to be fitting examples because they capture two crucial ingredients of teamwork: concertion and faith. Without those two ingredients, true teamwork ceases to exist.

Concertion is the act of *concerting* or deliberately adjusting your behaviors to be *in concert* (in sync) with those around you. In the sport of rowing, team members must row *in concert* with each other. They must match the speed, strength, and rhythm of their fellow rowers.

For their boat to achieve maximum efficiency, rowers can't necessarily row as fast as they want or can, nor are they able to slow down to a pace that is comfortable to them. Concertion requires rowers to sacrifice their comfort and desire to row differently than the rest of their team. They must adjust their *wants* to meet their teams' *needs*.

A popular African proverb advises: *If you want to go fast, go alone; if you want to go far, go together.* Rowing simultaneously rebuts and affirms that proverb. No kayak nor canoe can move faster nor farther than a team of rowers.

Kayaking and canoeing provide a contrasting illustration of the second crucial teamwork ingredient. In kayaking and canoeing you face forward and can see where the boat is heading. That's not the case with rowing.

In rowing, everyone but the coxswain (leader) is facing backwards. Rowing requires faith. Rowers must trust the vision of their leader and believe that their individual efforts are contributing to the boat heading in the right direction.

Concertion and faith lead to synergy—the product of combined efforts yielding greater results than the sum of individual efforts. Good teammates practice both concertion and faith.

We've all experienced occasions when we've wanted to "do our own thing"—on our own schedule and at our own pace. But when you are part of a team, you aren't afforded that kind of independence. You need to adapt to your teams' schedule and pace.

Being part of a team necessitates *give-and-take*. Sometimes you are going to need to give more than you expect; other times you will need to take on less than you want. In either situation, you must have faith that your *giving* or *taking* is advancing your team.

The need for concertion and faith may not be apparent when merrily rowing the boat down gently flowing streams. But they are imperative when the team is challenged by the proverbial rough waters—and every goal-driven team faces challenges at some point. The value of true teamwork, and truly good teammates, is revealed during these moments.

As always…Good teammates care. Good teammates share. Good teammates listen. Go be a good teammate.

5

When the Tooth Fairy Fails
MAY 25

The tooth fairy failed. Epically. Twice.

When I'm not traveling for speaking engagements, I have a morning routine that I try to follow. I wake up, drink a small bottle of water, eat a quick breakfast, brush my teeth, and then head into my home office to do some work before the rest of my family gets up.

I've discovered myself to be particularly productive during this time. My circadian rhythms are optimized and the stillness of the house minimizes the chances of me getting distracted.

Yesterday morning, I had my office door shut when my youngest daughter barged in. We don't have a lot of rules in our house when it comes to me working at home. I generally leave my office door open.

Anyone is welcome to enter and interrupt whatever I'm doing if my door is open. But if my door is closed, that means

I'm doing something important and they know not to enter unless it's an emergency.

I immediately knew something was wrong when the door swung open and I saw my teary-eyed daughter holding a baggie in her hand.

"I put my tooth under my pillow last night, but the Tooth Fairy didn't come," she said.

A blizzard of emotions engulfed me—shame, embarrassment, disappointment, anger, etc. My daughter had lost one of her final baby teeth. How could the Tooth Fairy have forgotten such a monumental occasion?

I started to make excuses for the Tooth Fairy: *Maybe the Tooth Fairly was really busy last night. Maybe the Tooth Fairy tried to come when you were still awake. Did you stay up too late? Maybe the Tooth Fairy didn't see your tooth. Are you sure you put it in the right place?*

But those were just feeble excuses for inexcusable behavior. The tooth fairy failed, *epically*, and needed to own that mistake.

When good teammates make mistakes, their initial response should be to take responsibility for their actions. Don't waste time making excuses or trying to deflect blame. Own the mistake, apologize, and commit to righting the error.

I stopped trying to make excuses for the Tooth Fairy and shifted my focus to consoling my daughter. Thankfully, she agreed to put her tooth back under her pillow and give it another try.

My office door swung open again this morning, and I again saw my daughter standing in the doorway. She didn't have any tears on her face this time. However, she did have a look of disappointment. She was holding cash in one hand and what looked like a note in the other—along with the same baggie from the day before.

"Well, the Tooth Fairy came last night, Daddy. She left me some money and an apology note but forgot to take my tooth."

I cringed as my daughter held up the baggie containing her tooth.

When my daughter told my wife what happened, my wife looked at me and smirked. She then proceeded to cryptically state that she would like to send the Tooth Fairy a text that included a deserving *you-had-one-job* gif.

I cringed again.

The Tooth Fairy had failed for the second time in as many days. As I contemplated what to say about the situation, my daughter offered her thoughts:

"You know, the Tooth Fairy has been good to me and never made mistakes like this before. I think we should give the Tooth Fairy a break," she said. "But if it happens again, I'm going to write Santa a letter and recommend he put the Tooth Fairy on the naughty list."

I was satisfied with that recommendation.

How the Tooth Fairy responded to the first mistake is an example of how you should respond to making a mistake (*own it, apologize, and commit to righting the error*). How my daughter responded to the second mistake is an example of how you should respond to an established good teammate making a mistake.

Temper your emotions, consider the value of their past contributions, cut them a break, and tactfully remind them of the consequences should their mistake happen to be repeated. No further discipline nor action is required.

Responding in this manner will be a good teammate move on your part that I am CERTAIN the offending party will appreciate.

As always…Good teammates care. Good teammates share. Good teammates listen. Go be a good teammate.

Givers, Takers, Shakers, and Bakers
JUNE 1

The best machines are comprised of the best components. The best cars have the best engines, transmissions, headlights, etc. The best computers have the best processors, keyboards, monitors, etc.

Teams are a lot like machines in that they too are comprised of components—teammates. Here are four types of teammates you should have on your team:

1. THE GIVER

Who They Are: Givers are generous. They share their gifts with their teammates. Giving their time and energy to their team is standard practice. With givers, it's never "my" time; it's always "our" time. Their willingness to give freely of themselves is a clear indication of their devotion to their team. Givers also give credit when and where credit is due. They are the first to recognize and praise other teammates' contributions. Givers share the spotlight. They are never jealous of another team member's achievements.

Their Benefit to the Team: Givers facilitate trust. No one questions the purity of a giver's motives because they know givers are driven by love. They selflessly serve the needs of their teams.

2. THE TAKER

Who They Are: Takers take ownership of their responsibilities. They take their role on the team seriously by holding themselves and everyone else on the team accountable. They don't make excuses or blame others for their mistakes. Takers will never throw another teammate under the bus to save themselves. Takers also take initiative. When they see something that needs done, they dive in with eagerness. Takers don't have to be "voluntold."

Their Benefit to the Team: Takers facilitate loyalty. Their example builds team cohesion and inspires commitment. Their actions lead to positive change.

3. THE SHAKER

Who They Are: Shakers are enthusiastic. Think up-beat Latin music. Think maracas, tambourines, and cowbells. Shakers energize their teams. They invigorate others and compel teammates to shake their tail feathers. Shakers also shake things up. They get teams out of ruts by introducing new routines and embracing new strategies. They keep their teams from becoming stagnant.

Their Benefit to the Team: Shakers facilitate momentum. Their energy and enthusiasm are catalysts for action. Shakers prevent complacency.

4. THE BAKER

Who They Are: Bakers are dependable. They're good listeners who follow instructions with precision. The best bakeries have consistently good products because the individuals preparing those products follow the recipes with great diligence. Bakers are thorough. They pay attention to details and never skip steps. Bakers also give more than what is required. Think "baker's dozen." When others are content to meet expectations, bakers push themselves to exceed them.

Their Benefit to the Team: Bakers facilitate the implementation of game plans. They successfully transfer instructions into action. Their ability to listen and respond minimizes miscues.

The difference between a machine's components versus a team's is exclusivity. An engine can only be an engine. A keyboard can only be a keyboard. The components of a team are not confined by those restrictions. A teammate can exhibit all the above behaviors at the same time.

The best teams are comprised of individuals who are simultaneously givers, takers, shakers, and bakers. Being a teammate who is worthy of all four labels should be your objective.

As always…Good teammates care. Good teammates share. Good teammates listen. Go be a good teammate.

7

Upsy Daisy
JUNE 8

According to the registrar of all that is worthy of celebration, The National Day Calendar, tomorrow is officially National Upsy Daisy Day—a day to "get up gloriously, gratefully and gleefully."

Upsy Daisy is such a whimsical expression. It's both fun to say and hear. Though typically used to reassure a child who has fallen down, *upsy daisy* can also be a lighthearted way of encouraging an adult to persevere.

The expression's exact origins are unknown, though it is probably safe to assume they are at least partially derived from the idea of rising up after being on the ground *among the daisies.* Historically, daisies are associated with new beginnings.

Symbolically, the flower itself plays into the expression's meaning. Known as "the day's eye," the daisy closes at night but opens to expose its magnificent yellow center when hit by sunlight. The daisy doesn't just open, it opens with radiance.

Telling someone *upsy daisy* is a way of hitting that person with a dose of positivity and helping them reset their attitude.

Helping others is a mark of a teammate who cares. In my children's book, *Be a Good Teammate,* I illustrate the concept of caring with a drawing of a player extending a hand to help a fallen teammate. The caption on the page reads: *If my teammate falls down, I help her up.*

Good teammates never rejoice in a fellow teammate's failures. When someone on their team stumbles, they see it as their duty to pick their teammate up—sometimes literally, sometimes figuratively. In either case, they must be sure to pick their teammate up the right way.

During nursing school clinicals, students are taught early how to safely lift a patient. They learn that using the wrong technique can result in them hurting the patient and/or themselves. The same is true for good teammates.

If your approach to lifting a fallen teammate is to take over their responsibilities and do their job for them, you risk becoming an enabler. This response will lead to repeated missteps, promote the continuation of ill-advised behaviors, and do your teammate (and your team) a disservice. A better approach is to follow what nurses are taught:

- Keep a firm base and maintain balance.
- Avoid twisting your body or getting your head and neck out of alignment.
- Keep the person who is being lifted close to your body and lift with your whole body.
- Encourage the patient to help you help them.

For good teammates, those instructions translate to mean:

- Stay true to your principles.
- Don't compromise your integrity in your efforts to help.
- Don't dabble in helping them from a distance; be fully immersed in your service.
- Encourage your teammate to help you help them.

Sometimes the best way to help a fallen teammate is to become their biggest cheerleader. Whether you tell them *you can do it, keep fighting,* or *upsy daisy,* know that your encouraging words can be just the help your teammate needed.

As always…Good teammates care. Good teammates share. Good teammates listen. Go be a good teammate.

Strength in Numbers
JUNE 15

Nature is a marvelous teacher. So many great lessons about teamwork can be learned by observing wildlife interactions. I recently witnessed an encounter between a "team" of purple martins and a much larger predator that demonstrated an important good-teammate trait.

Purple martins are migratory swallows. These tiny birds make the more than 6,000 mile trek from Brazil to Canada every year. As they journey north, the purple martins stop in central Florida to nest for a few weeks between late January and early June.

About twenty years ago, Walt Disney World began erecting purple martin birdhouses around its properties, as the birds are not only fascinating to watch but also helpful with insect control.

Disney partnered with Microsoft in 2018 to design smart birdhouses—gourd-shaped enclosures specially equipped with environmental sensors and HD cameras. The objective was to study the birds' "secret lives."

As I have previously written, I live near Disney World. My neighbor is a Disney Conservation cast member, and he set up a purple martin birdhouse in our neighborhood. I was walking by it the other day when a much larger hawk tried to access the nests.

What ensued was a display of aerial combat like I had never before seen. Dozens of purple martins swarmed the hawk. Though considerably smaller, the purple martins were relentless in their defense. They attacked the hawk from every imaginable angle. No matter what path the hawk took, the purple martins blocked it.

In defending their birdhouse, the purple martins proved the merits of there being strength in numbers. The hawk was bigger, stronger, and faster than any single purple martin. But he was no match for them all working together.

The "strength in numbers" advantage only applies if each member of the team is fully committed. If at any time, the members become fearful and revert to self-preservation, the advantage is immediately negated.

Had one of the purple martins caved to fear, the hawk would have exploited the opening and broken through the defense. But like good teammates, the purple martins held firm.

Good teammates resist the natural urge to revert to self-preservation. They don't *give in* nor *give up*, even when those options seem to be the safer, more logical choice. By remaining faithful and courageous, they don't succumb to the reality of their individual inferiority.

When the hawk finally flew away, the purple martins nonchalantly returned to their prior behaviors. In doing so, they demonstrated another noble good-teammate trait: humility.

They did their jobs without boasting, posturing, or fanfare. They worked together because that's what their team expected of them. The purple martins unwaveringly put "we" in front "me."

As always…Good teammates care. Good teammates share. Good teammates listen. Go be a good teammate.

Details about Walt Disney World's smart birdhouses is from Briggs, Bill. "Magic of nature: Disney's Smart Birdhouses Reveal the Secret Lives of Purple Martins." June 18, 2018. https://news.microsoft.com/transform/disneys-smart-birdhouses-reveal-the-secret-lives-of-purple-martins/

Eight Off-Season Good Teammate Habits
JUNE 22

Anyone who is part of a team experiences an "off-season"—a lull in activity, a break from the monotony, a calm before the next storm. For sports teams, the off-season occurs between the end of one season and the start of the next. For teachers and educational teams, it takes place over summer break. For corporate teams, the off-season may not be as formally defined. It could be the end of a fiscal quarter or the period following tax time.

Whatever the case may be, what individual members of these respective teams do during this span influences their next "season." Here are eight off-season habits of good teammates that set their teams up for future success:

1. **They assess.** Good teammates possess the humility to take a retrospective look at their performance from last season. They objectively evaluate what they did well, and what they didn't. They don't dwell on their

past failures, nor their past victories, but they do make an effort to recognize both.

2. **They recharge and reboot.** Good teammates understand the toll the intensity of the previous "season" had on their minds and bodies. They devote specific time to rest and engage in fun, stress-free activities that hasten mental and physical recovery before moving onto the next season.

3. **They set new objectives.** Good teammates not only possess the humility to look back, but they also have the courage to look forward. They don't rest on their laurels, accept defeat, or maintain the status quo. They are intentional about identifying objectives that will lead to prosperity.

4. **They invest in personal development.** Good teammates actively engage in opportunities to grow their knowledge. They find ways to improve upon their current skills and develop new skills. This may come from attending a conference, enrolling in a course, or hiring a personal trainer.

5. **They include other team members.** Good teammates are driven by team success, not individual success. They make certain to include other team members in personal development opportunities. They invite others to join them in training to get better—and they don't accept no for an answer.

6. **They continue to script their time.** Good teammates appreciate how tight their schedules are during the season. They don't allow the freedom of the off-season to cause them to become lazy and lapse in their time management. They continue to plan their day with diligence.

7. **They stay connected.** Good teammates maintain contact with other team members throughout the off-season. Some time away from each other can be beneficial, but too much weakens the bond. They strategically keep this from happening by communicating through random social media messages, texts, emails, and brief phone calls.

8. **They form new relationships.** Good teammates use the off-season to expand their field of influence. They reach out to individuals outside of their normal circle who may be knowledgeable in subjects about which they know little. Likewise, they seek to share their expertise with novices who may be less knowledgeable.

How do you approach your off-season? Do you incorporate the above habits into your approach? Good teammates must be forward thinking and see the off-season as the time to lay the framework for their teams' success.

As always…Good teammates care. Good teammates share. Good teammates listen. Go be a good teammate.

Depleted, Not Defeated
JUNE 29

This year, Father's Day fell on my wife's birthday. We wanted to celebrate the occasions jointly by doing something out of the ordinary, like witnessing a "majestic" sight.

We couldn't decide which would be more majestic: watching a beach sunrise or a beach sunset. So we decided to try to see both—on the same day.

There are only a handful of places in the world where doing this is possible without getting on a plane, our home state of Florida being one of them. We woke up in the predawn hours, sat on a dark beach, and watched the sunrise on the Atlantic coast. We then hopped into our car, drove west, and enjoyed a few hours of beach time before watching the sunset on the Gulf coast.

The experience was truly majestic and one that we will remember for many years to come.

When I was a kid, my grandmother had a bronze statue on her mantel. The statue was similar to James Earle Fraser's iconic "End of the Trail" sculpture in that it depicted an exhausted Native American warrior slumped over a declining, weary horse.

A corresponding statue resided on the mantel at my aunt's house, only hers depicted an invigorated Native American warrior perched atop a rearing, energetic horse. My aunt's statue was titled "Sunrise" and my grandmother's "Sunset."

I always thought those two pieces illustrated the bookends of a noble day. The more I study the art of being a good teammate, the more I realize they illustrate the daily journey of a good teammate.

Like the warrior in my aunt's statue, good teammates rise each morning, ready to attack the day with enthusiasm. They may not know what challenges await them, but they are excited to serve the needs of their team.

Good teammates don't begrudgingly ease into their day. They aren't bitter. They aren't still holding onto the yesterday's baggage. They aren't grouchy until they "get their coffee."

Good teammates are, quite literally, raring to go. Why? Because that is the type of selfless, enthusiastic approach that their team needs.

As much as the "Sunrise" statue illustrates the start of a good teammate's day, the "Sunset" statue may illustrate an even more accurate ending. Good teammates put their all into serving their teams' needs. They expunge every ounce of their energy, effort, and enthusiasm. They exhaust themselves—*for their teams*.

Their endings should be interpreted as depleted, not defeated. This distinction explains why good teammates are able to go to bed with a clear conscience. They know they fought the good fight, withheld nothing in doing so, and accept the impending need to do it all over again the tomorrow.

Good teammates sleep soundly, rise enthusiastically, and fight courageously. Their cycle reminds us that it is impossible to defeat someone who never gives up. You might say, good teammates never let the sun set on their devotion to their team.

As always…Good teammates care. Good teammates share. Good teammates listen. Go be a good teammate.

11

Putting Who First
JULY 6

Several noteworthy events occurred on this date in history: Richard "The Lionheart" was crowned King of England (1186) as was Richard III (1483), the notorious pirate Captain William Kidd was finally captured (1699), Babe Ruth hit the first-ever homerun in the first-ever MLB All Star game (1933), and *The Naughty Nineties* made its theatrical debut (1945).

The significance of that last event may not seem as obvious as the others. *The Naughty Nineties* didn't win any Oscars, nor did it fair particularly well at the box office. It wasn't even one of the top 100 grossing films for that year.

But the film is nonetheless noteworthy because it included what *Time* called "The Best Comedy Routine of the Twentieth Century"—Abbott and Costello's *Who's on First*.

Bud Abbott and Lou Costello had been performing their signature skit for years on stage and radio. *The Naughty Nineties* marked the first time the full version of *Who's on*

First appeared on film. This now-famous movie clip plays continuously at the Baseball Hall of Fame in Cooperstown, NY.

Abbot and Costello are a great example of teammates using their differences as assets to advance a common objective.

Abbott was tall and slender. He had a deep, mature, masculine voice. He was neat and together. Contrastingly, Costello was short and pudgy, spoke in a high-pitched voice, and often looked disheveled. Yet their differences were eclipsed by a commitment to a common objective that facilitated their chemistry—make the audience laugh.

The tandem's comedic success stemmed from their ability to play off their differences. Abbott's *straight-lacedness* provided the perfect balance to Costello's *tomfoolery*, and vice versa.

Sometimes team members get wrapped up in comparisons. They get frustrated by their differences instead of embracing their commonality. When teammates prioritize their shared commitment to their teams' primary objective, their differences can become assets rather than liabilities.

For example, the thoroughness of the team's methodical plodder can prevent the high-energy go-getter from hurting the team with an overzealous mistake. Similarly, the team's stoic can remain objective and prevent the team's nurturer from making emotional decisions.

Being a good teammate means recognizing and valuing the different talents other team members bring to your team, especially when those talents are different than yours.

It is serendipitous that Abbott and Costello put Who on first and What on second, because that is what good teammates do: They put their *who* first and their *what* second. A good teammate's *who* is their team, and their *what* is their self-serving agenda.

In the Abbott and Costello skit, *Who* is on first, *What* is on second, and *I Don't Know* is on third. When teammates put their *who* first and their *what* second, I do know the entity that follows—*team success*.

As always...Good teammates care. Good teammates share. Good teammates listen. Go be a good teammate.

*The full Abbott and Costello "Who's on First" skit can be viewed at https://www.youtube.com/watch?v=sShMA85pv8M.

12

The Parachute Packer Standard
JULY 13

When I am working with a team, I will sometimes ask the members, "Is *so-and-so* (an individual on that team) a good teammate?" The response is usually a resounding "yes!"

I then ask a follow-up question that can reveal a lot about their teams' cultures: "If you were jumping out of a plane, would you trust *so-and-so* (the same individual) to pack your parachute?"

Many of those who said *so-and-so* was a good teammate reply that they would not trust that individual to pack their parachutes.

When I ask them why that is, they often attempt to tell me it's because *so-and-so* doesn't know anything about skydiving or parachutes. That may be a valid point, but their explanation, in my experience, is a red herring, diverting attention away from another issue.

To counter their excuse and move closer to the truth, I'll stipulate: "What if we sent *so-and-so* to training school and got them certified on how to properly pack a parachute before they packed yours, then would you trust them?"

A surprising number continue to decline.

Packing a parachute is actually a relatively simple process. Experienced skydivers do it in about fifteen minutes. An Army YouTube video teaches viewers how to do it in less than one minute.

I concede that while packing a parachute may be a simple process, dereliction can have grave consequences. Entrusting someone to pack your parachute requires a deep level of trust. You need to know that—without exception—you can depend on that individual to be diligent in their responsibilities.

The same is true when it comes to the criteria for good teammates. My questions above are intended to demonstrate how misguided the standards are on some teams. Underperforming teams are filled with members who think someone they can't trust to be diligent is a "good teammate."

Trust is the cornerstone of a healthy team culture. Having a deep level of trust between team members leads to growth, accountability, effective communication, and psychological safety.

If you can't trust a team member to pack your parachute, then one of you is not a good teammate. Either they haven't proven themselves trustworthy or you have detrimental trust issues. Whichever the case may be, your team is not going to reach its potential until that situation is remedied.

Successful teams value trust and infuse it into the standards of their culture. Trust is what keeps teams from suffering grave consequences.

It doesn't matter how likable, friendly, charming, funny, or generous you are; you must also be trustworthy to be considered a good teammate. Your fellow team members must know they can depend upon you to be diligent in your responsibilities.

As always…Good teammates care. Good teammates share. Good teammates listen. Go be a good teammate.

The Army YouTube video reference above can be viewed at https://www.youtube.com/watch?v=3uZEAD27zY0

Big Frank's Morning Beverage
JULY 20

I was waiting in line the other day at Starbucks when a barista called out the name "Frank." A large, burly man with a bushy beard approached the counter.

With an obvious look of dread on her face, the barista informed Frank that they were out of the drink he had ordered.

The store was packed, and the staff had been contending with difficult, impatient customers all morning. In a deep bellowing voice, Frank replied, "Is that so?"

I sensed that the barista was preparing herself for an impending *Karen-esque* confrontation. You can imagine her relief when Frank continued, "Ehh, no big deal. Just give me something else fruity. You pick it."

Those of us waiting in line who overheard the exchange couldn't help but chuckle at Frank's unexpected response. As the barista left to prepare his alternative selection, I joked with Frank that he sure was hard to get along with.

In the same deep bellowing voice, Frank said, "You know, there are just some things you can't control. If you're going to get bent out of shape over your choice in morning beverages, the rest of your day is going to be a real struggle."

What a refreshing perspective! So many of us allow our days to be derailed by trivial inconveniences over which we have no control.

As Robert Fulghum, bestselling author of *All I Really Need to Know I Learned in Kindergarten*, said: "One of life's best coping mechanisms is to know the difference between an inconvenience and a problem. If you break your neck, if you have nothing to eat, if your house is on fire—then you've got a problem. Everything else is an inconvenience."

Good teammates recognize the difference between a problem and an inconvenience. When teammates confuse inconveniences for problems, they create unnecessary drama. They cause stress for themselves and everyone else on their team.

Frank and I struck up a conversation on our way out of Starbucks. He told me that he works in construction and spends most of his days dealing with "whiny contractors."

"They complain about everything" Frank said. "But I can't control the weather and backorders. They all think that if they complain enough, their issues will go away."

Although, sometimes their strategy works. Because if they complain too much, I just stop doing business with them. Bam! The issues go away."

People often try to justify incessant complaining with the expression "The wheel that squeaks the loudest gets the oil."

That logic might be temporarily applicable. But, like Frank's "whiny contractors," the squeaky wheel eventually gets replaced—and rightfully so.

A big part of being a good teammate is not allowing yourself to become a team problem. Incessant complaining about inconveniences will ensure your failure at this objective. The better strategy is to follow Frank's example and not get bent out of shape over the trivial "things" which you cannot control.

As always...Good teammates care. Good teammates share. Good teammates listen. Go be a good teammate.

When Individuals Inspire
JULY 27

After a year's long delay, the Games of the XXXII Olympiad are officially underway in Tokyo!

For generations, the Olympics have been a source of inspiration. In fact, some of the most inspirational feats in sports history have occurred during the Olympics:

- Jesse Owens winning four gold medals in front of Adolph Hitler during the 1936 Berlin Olympics

- Ethiopian Abebe Bikila running an entire marathon barefoot to win gold during the 1960 Rome Olympics

- Fourteen-year-old Romanian Nadia Comaneci becoming the first female gymnast to score a perfect "10" during the 1976 Montreal Olympics

- Michael Johnson breaking two world records and becoming the first ever sprinter to win gold medals in both the 100m and 200m during the 1996 Atlanta Olympics

- Kerri Strug, despite injuring her ankle on her previous attempt, sticking the landing on her final vault during the 1996 Atlanta Olympics

- Michael Phelps setting a record by winning eight gold medals during the 2008 Beijing Olympics and becoming the most decorated Olympian of all time with twenty-eight total medals during the 2016 Rio de Janeiro Olympics

I can attest personally to being inspired by an Olympic performance. If you've read my book *The WE Gear*, you know that its title was inspired by something that occurred during the 2016 Rio de Janeiro Olympics. After setting an Olympic record for rebounds, USA men's basketball player DeAndre Jordan used the word "we" an abundance of times in his postgame interview.

While DeAndre Jordan's Olympic performance was connected to a team sport, it was his actions as an individual that inspired me. The same is largely true for all the performances listed above.

I am occasionally asked, "How does the art of being a good teammate apply to athletes participating in individual sports like golf, running, and tennis?" Apart from special competitions like the Davis Cup or the Olympics where individual scores are tallied towards a team score, success in these sports is gauged on an individual basis.

Whenever someone asks me how the art of being a good teammate applies to individual sports, my response is: If your individual actions inspire others, then you're somebody's teammate. And as such, you have a responsibility to be a good teammate.

For individual sport athletes, being a good teammate translates into being ultra-aware of how they conduct themself. They show loyalty by not allowing those who admire them to be let down through disappointing efforts or dishonorable actions. Their example is everything.

As always...Good teammates care. Good teammates share. Good teammates listen. Go be a good teammate.

15

Stay-In-Your-Lane Teammates
AUGUST 3

Do you have *stay-in-your-lane teammates* on your team? If your team is underachieving, you likely do.

As the label suggests, stay-in-your-lane teammates don't venture from their lane—i.e., their comfort zone. They're content to keep to themselves, mind their own business, and stick to what they know.

They don't bother anyone on the team; but they don't go out of their way to help anyone, either.

They don't cause any problems; but they don't try to solve any, either.

Stay-in-your-lane teammates are not bad teammates; but they are not necessarily good teammates, either. And without good teammates, teams fall short of their potential.

The main issue with stay-in-your-lane teammates is that the lane they're in leads to mediocrity. Their way of thinking keeps teams from experiencing growth.

These individuals tend to construct silos that prevent collaboration. They don't like to be challenged or inconvenienced. Their aversion to operating outside of their comfort zones interrupts teamwork and makes it hard for teams to pursue bigger goals.

I acknowledge that occasions exist where being a good teammate can equate to staying in your lane. If you think of the expression's meaning from the perspective of focusing on your role and not worrying about everyone else's, then sure, staying in your lane can be good.

In that same context, staying in your lane can be beneficial in terms of averting comparisons and thwarting jealousy—two elements that divide teams.

But for a team to grow, staying in your lane cannot be your only method of operation. You must also be willing to pass and yield.

Passing means confronting with action. If your team is entangled in toxicity or succumbing to apathy, staying in your lane will not change the situation. You need to muster the courage to change lanes and accelerate.

Making a deeper commitment, taking on more responsibilities, assuming a leadership role, or abandoning a clique are actions that accelerate growth and move the team in a more positive direction.

Yielding means suppressing your ego. Sometimes the fastest way forward for the team is for the individual to back off or move aside. Delegating responsibilities, empowering others, or demonstrating humility by engaging in work that might be beneath you can also lead to team growth.

When teammates yield their ego to their team, they clear the path to team success.

Anyone who has ever driven on a busy multi-lane highway knows that driving in a middle lane can seem safer and less stressful. But staying in your lane while others consistently zoom by you on both sides can be dangerous—for you and them.

Erratically speeding around everyone else or not allowing other drivers to merge can be comparably dangerous. Being a good teammate means being willing to stay in your lane, pass, and yield. And recognizing when to do each.

As always…Good teammates care. Good teammates share. Good teammates listen. Go be a good teammate.

Where We Cannot Take Ourselves
AUGUST 10

While *Teammate Tuesdays* has an overarching theme, I try to provide variety with the topics that fall within that theme. I realize that I wrote about the Olympics two weeks ago, but the Olympics are a special event. And as such, I feel they are deserving of an exception and worthy of a second mention.

This week, I want to highlight my favorite "good teammate" moment from the Tokyo Olympics. It happened Thursday during the final event of the men's decathlon—the 1500m.

Although the grueling ten-event decathlon is an individual competition, Australia's Ash Moloney was propelled to a bronze medal finish by an incredible *good teammate move* on the part of fellow countryman Cedric Dubler.

Moloney entered the 1500m only a few points ahead of American Garrett Scantling and Canadian Pierce LePage in the decathlon standings. He didn't need to beat Scantling or Pierce in the final event, but he did need to finish high enough to ensure he earned sufficient points to hold onto the bronze.

When Scantling pulled away from him on the final lap, an exhausted Moloney felt his chances of appearing on the podium fading. That's when Dubler appeared at Moloney's side.

"I just heard (Dubler's) voice in my brain and it filled me with energy," Moloney told media after the race.

Dubler relentlessly shouted encouragement as he ran alongside Moloney. He refused to allow Moloney to falter.

"My job was to get (Moloney) through it and keep track of where everyone was and make sure he collected that bronze," Dubler said. "I was screaming at him so loud in that last 300 that I had to kind of stop to keep screaming."

Dubler may have already been out of contention for a decathlon medal. But by helping his teammate win a medal, he sacrificed his own 1500m finish and a chance to improve his individual overall standing. He chose "we" (his team) instead of "me" (himself).

Until Thursday's event, no Australian decathlete had ever finished higher than sixth in an Olympic competition. Every once in a while, the sports world gets it right when it comes to praise. Cedric Dubler is rightfully being celebrated as a hero for his selfless action. Perhaps the reason is that everyone of us knows how valuable it can be to have a teammate by our side who energizes us when we are struggling.

An Airbnb-sponsored commercial featuring Paralympic champion Blake Leeper aired during the Tokyo Games. In the commercial, Leeper describes coming up short by trying to do it all by himself. He explains that it wasn't until he embraced the help of his team that he was able to overcome the adversity that was holding him back.

The message in Leeper's commercial compliments the lesson derived from Moloney's race: *Good teammates can take us where we cannot take ourselves.* They can be the fuel that powers the seemingly impossible.

I happen to believe that we can all benefit from having an encouraging teammate, and that we also all have it within us to be someone else's encouraging teammate. In the words of Booker T. Washington, "If you want to lift yourself up, lift up someone else."

As always…Good teammates care. Good teammates share. Good teammates listen. Go be a good teammate.

*Cedric Dubler's quote is from Salvaldo, John. "Bronze Medal for Ash Moloney in Decathlon." August 8, 2021. https://7news.com.au/sport/athletics/bronze-medal-for-ash-moloney-in-decathlon-c-3606999

Ten Ways to Be a Good Back-to-School Teammate
AUGUST 17

Can you believe it's already back-to-school time? The return to school this year will undoubtedly present a unique set of challenges—the sort of challenges that are best faced by adopting a good teammate's mindset.

Here are ten ways for both students and teachers to be good back-to-school teammates:

1. **Exhibit patience.** Enter the year expecting the unexpected. Teams are rarely in sync when they are coming off prolonged periods of disconnect. No matter what challenges arise, be patient. You don't have to abandon your commitment to excellence, but you may need to temporarily defer it for the sake of the team.

2. **Practice punctuality.** In general, being on time and keeping on schedule are good teammate practices. But at the start of the school year, punctuality is addedly important. School leaders are already overburdened with stress. You can alleviate some of their stress by arriving extra early to functions and giving them one less thing to worry about.

3. **Share resources.** Can you lend a pencil to a classmate who doesn't have one? Can you lend some classroom supplies to a teaching colleague who doesn't have enough? Willingly sharing resources strengthens teammate connections.

4. **Share knowledge.** Good teammates share more than their resources. What knowledge have you acquired through experience? Sharing your experience with a new student or new staff member can accelerate their assimilation into the team.

5. **Look for loners.** Good teammates leave no teammate behind! Be on the lookout for individuals sitting alone, eating lunch by themselves, or otherwise not being included. Go out of your way to make those individuals feel welcome by introducing them to your group and getting them involved in what you're doing.

6. **Model behavior.** Your example is everything. Unfamiliarity can be frightening. Those who aren't

sure how to handle unfamiliarity may model their behavior after you. How you look, speak, think, and act matters. Make sure your example is worth emulating.

7. **Follow instructions.** Listen intently to instructions and do your best to follow them with precision—especially in the beginning of the year. This is not the time to listen halfheartedly or distractedly. Focus lays the groundwork for an accelerated future.

8. **Learn Expectations.** View learning what is expected of you as your responsibility. Ideally, the team's leadership would convey expectations to you, but they may be too preoccupied with other issues to be able to do so. Take it upon yourself to learn what they specifically expect of you and do your best to comply.

9. **Divulge Details.** Trust leads to team success. Allowing yourself to be vulnerable and tactfully divulging details about your life is a way to build trust through familiarity. We trust who we know. Have the courage to share your life with others.

10. **Extend kindness.** When you care, you're kind. The kindness and empathy you convey today may be what keeps someone from breaking tomorrow. Kindness is found in stepping outside of your comfort zone, inconveniencing yourself for another,

and making sacrifices for the greater good. Kindness leads to kinship.

May the school year get off to a good start for every student, teacher, parent, and administrator. I hope you find fulfillment in your respective endeavors and that you are all able to be good back-to-school teammates.

As always…Good teammates care. Good teammates share. Good teammates listen. Go be a good teammate.

Harold the Shuttle Bus Driver
AUGUST 24

Travel can be incredibly stressful, especially air travel. A lot of my time lately has been spent passing through airports on my way to speaking engagements.

Air travel is laden with stress. Some passengers fear flying. Some are overwhelmed by the confusing TSA security procedures. Others are anxious about delays, missed connections, and lost luggage.

The cumulation of these stressors can lead to unpleasant encounters between passengers and airport staff that may not happen under less stressful conditions. For airport staff, the situation is akin to dealing with individuals suffering from hangriness.

Until *hangry* individuals eat, they are irritable, irrational, and easily agitated. In traveling, the over-stressed don't need to be fed food; they need to be fed happiness.

It behooves airport leadership to place good teammates— those gifted with the ability to feed others happiness—in positions where friction between staff and stressed travelers is most likely to occur. Their placement reduces tension. A recent encounter with a shuttle bus driver named Harold reminded me of this fact.

I had just dropped off my rental car and was rushing to catch the shuttle to take me to the terminal. As I neared the pick-up spot, I watched the shuttle bus start to pull away. I was already running late and stressed about missing my flight. Having to wait another twenty minutes for the next shuttle did not thrill me.

The driver must have saw me hustling toward the pick-up spot. To my surprise, he stopped the bus, backed up, and waited on me. Words cannot express how much I appreciated his kindness and understanding.

Once I caught my breath and settled into my seat, I realized that I was the only passenger on the bus, which made the driver's gesture even more appreciated. The driver, a thin, middle-aged African American man named Harold, asked me if I minded if he "turned up the tunes." After what he had just done for me, I obviously had no objections.

For the second time in as many minutes, Harold surprised me. He proceeded to sing along with the song on the radio— Frank Sinatra's "Mack the Knife."

Harold unabashedly belted out the lyrics. His enthusiasm and clear zeal for life put a smile on my face. When I exited his shuttle, I wasn't stressed about missing my flight or anything else for that matter. I was happy and grateful for life's unexpected gifts.

Traveling has caused me to unfortunately witness the worst of humanity and, occasionally (like my encounter with Harold the Shuttle Bus Driver), allowed me to experience the best.

I happen to be a genuine Frank Sinatra fan. I like "Mack the Knife." The song's upbeat, but it's about a murderer and doesn't exactly carry a joyous meaning. I am fonder of Old Blue Eyes' "When You're Smiling." The opening lines of "When You're Smiling" express the emotional contagiousness of a good teammate's attitude:

> *When you're smilin', the whole word smiles with you.*
> *When you're laughin', the sun comes shinin' through.*

Being cognizant of the potential effect your emotions have on others is an important component of being a good teammate. You never know how deeply stepping outside of your comfort zone, sharing your vulnerabilities, or transmitting your positivity can impact someone else's life.

As always…Good teammates care. Good teammates share. Good teammates listen. Go be a good teammate.

Uneasy Is the Crown, But Not Heavy
AUGUST 31

"Heavy is the head that wears the crown" is one of history's most misquoted lines. It's right up there with Darth Vader's "Luke, I am your father." (Darth Vader never uttered those words in any *Star Wars* movie. His actual line in *The Empire Strikes Back* was the rather less dramatic "No, I am your father.")

Like the Darth Vader misquote, "Heavy is the head that wears the crown" has entrenched itself into common vernacular. The expression, used to describe the burden of being a leader, comes from Shakespeare's *Henry IV, Part 2*. In the third act, the weary king complains about his inability to sleep, stating:

> *Canst thou, O partial sleep, give thy repose*
> *To the wet sea-boy in an hour so rude,*
> *And in the calmest and most stillest night,*
> *With all appliances and means to boot,*

Deny it to a king? Then happy low, lie down!
Uneasy lies the head that wears a crown.

With all the comforts surrounding him, in the middle of the quiet night, the king is still unable to fall asleep. Ordinary people do not ordinarily have this problem. As Shakespeare eloquently points out, even the lowly cabin boy traversing stormy waters can rest. So why can't the king?

I find it interesting that those with heavy eyes must fight to stay awake, yet those with heavy heads are unable to sleep. I suppose the reason is that heavy eyes come from fatigue; heavy heads come from responsibility. The reason for the king's insomnia? The weight of his worries.

Being a leader is not easy. When you are charged with responsibility—and you care—you worry about everything. *Am I making the right decision? Will my decision lead to backlash? What will others think of me?*

Outcomes, potential problems, and public perception all matter to you. And, to a degree, they should.

Because good teammates care so deeply about their teams and their fellow teammates, they share a similar burden. Only good teammates employ a mechanism that allows them to comfortably rest their heads at night.

Good teammates consistently make their decisions based on what is best for their team. That standard does not eliminate the weight of caring, nor does it abdicate them from the responsibility to care. But it does provide them with a sense of inner peace in that they know they made the best decision they could—*for their team.*

Be it leadership or being a good teammate, wearing the crown will never be easy. Anxiety will always accompany responsibility. Empathy will always be expected from you, yet seldom given to you. Your work will never seem done.

While wearing the crown may be uneasy, it does not have to be heavy. You can lighten the weight by choosing what is best for the team over what is best for the individual, not worrying about backlash, and not fretting over what others think of your decision.

Inner peace comes from ignoring the ignorance of outer opinions. Discover solace in the knowledge that your decisions served the needs of your team.

As always…Good teammates care. Good teammates share. Good teammates listen. Go be a good teammate.

20

Conceal, Feel, and Let Them Heal
SEPTEMBER 7

After much deliberation, my middle school-aged daughter decided to part ways with her Barbie dolls this week. She has amassed quite a collection over the years, but she doesn't play with them the way she used to.

Alas, it was, in her words, "Time to let 'em go."

As she sorted through her collection, she began setting a few dolls aside that she wanted to hold onto for various reasons (*This was the first Barbie I ever got. This one is a limited edition. I'm going to save this one to give to my daughter someday.*)

What began in her bedroom as a simple sorting process soon spread to a major operation in our living room. Dozens of Barbies, piles of doll clothes, and nearly every color and style of plastic shoe imaginable sprawled across the floor.

My daughter combed through the mess, painstakingly trying to match every individual doll with its original outfit. Her mother and I questioned her need to be so meticulous. If she was donating the dolls to charity, did it matter what clothes they had on? Did the dolls even need to be clothed?

Undeterred, she continued to sort. It occurred to me that her insistence on pairing the dolls with their original outfits was her way of saying goodbye. She was, in her own way, grieving.

Grieving can be triggered by any number of events. It is a natural emotional response to loss. In this case, my daughter was grieving the impending loss of her Barbie dolls—which represented the loss of a part of her childhood, her comfort zone, and her identity.

When you're part of a team, you may at some point find yourself in a position where you need to help a grieving teammate. Your teammate may be grieving over the death of a loved one, or they may be grieving over something that seems less significant to you, like a relationship breakup, a change in title or responsibilities, the realization of it being their final season, or a looming retirement. All of those "losses" equate to change, and change can be hard to handle. You can help a grieving teammate by doing the following:

Conceal. Your teammate may not be aware that their grieving is causing others grief. For instance, my daughter was oblivious to the anxiety and inconvenience her sprawling Barbie doll mess was causing her parents. Your teammate's grief may be creating a similar situation for you and the other members of your team.

If this is so, do your best to not let them become aware of the grief their grieving is causing others. They're experiencing enough stress as is, they don't need you compounding it. Accept that carrying an unbalanced load while they are grieving is a good teammate move and what is best for the team at this moment.

Feel. Practice intentional empathy. Imagine what it must feel like to be in your teammate's shoes. Their loss could be causing them to feel vulnerable and helpless, which could lead to their withdrawal. A bit of understanding on your part can help both of you cope with their grief.

On a side note, unless you have specifically gone through the identical experience, resist the urge to verbally commiserate with their grief. Though perhaps well intentioned, equating your experience to theirs may come across as insensitive and exacerbate the situation. Commit, instead, to maybe just being a good listener.

Let them heal. While they will likely progress through the fives stages of grief (denial, anger, bargaining, depression, and acceptance), there is no timetable for how long the process will take, nor an order to the way they will experience these stages—if they do at all.

Grieving is unique to each griever. Be patient with your teammate during the process. Let them know that you are willing and available to help them in whatever way you can, whenever they need.

People become loyal to those who were there to support them when they were at their lowest. Loyalty leads to trust and deep commitment—two attributes of good teammates.

Before my daughter dropped her last Barbie doll in the bin, she looked at me and said, "I'm done with the Barbies, but I'll always have the memories."

My heart smiled and I realized it was her who was being the good teammate. She was helping her parents get through the grief of watching their little girl grow up. *Good teammate move on her part.*

As always…Good teammates care. Good teammates share. Good teammates listen. Go be a good teammate.

Keep Scrolling Teammates
SEPTEMBER 14

A recent NBC News poll showed that 66% of adults log into some form of social media every day. I suspect that, if asked, 100% of that 66% would acknowledge seeing at least one post every day that draws their ire.

Social media can be a wonderful place for people to share their life, but it can also be a place for them to share their opinions—some of which may not align with yours. When you come upon posts of this nature, how do you respond?

With little discernment, many snap back with a reply contesting the poster's outrageousness.

I often find the outrageousness of those replies to be more outrageous than the original post. I wonder if the respondents knew that they were not required to comment. They could have chosen to simply keep scrolling.

Social media is designed to make the outrageous contagious. Algorithms reward posts that show a potential for engagement. Posts that demonstrate what the Pew Research

Center calls "indignant disagreement" receive nearly twice as much engagement as other types of content.

In other words, instigation is rewarded with attention.

I've written about the need for good teammates to confront toxic behaviors that threaten their teams' cultures on several previous occasions. And it's true, good teammates do need to possess the courage to confront toxic behaviors. But they must also possess the knowledge that choosing to not engage can be an effective confrontation strategy.

By hastily snapping back at posts that *draw your ire*, you risk fanning the flames and breathing life into something that would have otherwise died from an absence of attention.

In social media, your reply triggers the networks' algorithm and causes the post to be seen by more users. In the real world, engaging someone's inflammatory remarks can trigger gossip, unwanted attention, and drama—problems that can derail teams.

Good teammates avoid turning the petty into the profound by considering the possible outcomes of their response *before* they reply.

- *If I snap back, will my reply provide the instigator a platform that he or she may not currently have?*

- *Will my response amplify the instigator's influence over others?*

- *Will my response change the instigator's way of thinking?*

- *Is changing the instigator's way of thinking—on this particular issue—necessary for the success of our team?*

A little bit of consideration usually leads to the decision that the best option is to keep scrolling. The metaphorical swipe of a finger reduces team drama and turns *Keep Scrolling Teammates* into invaluable team assets.

Sometimes, being a good teammate means having the courage to confront and the wisdom to realize the best way to confront might be to not engage (i.e., just keep scrolling.).

As always…Good teammates care. Good teammates share. Good teammates listen. Go be a good teammate.

The NBC poll referenced above is from Murphy, Mark. "Poll: Nearly Two-Thirds of Americans Say Social Media Platforms Are Tearing Us Apart." May 9, 2021. https://www.nbcnews.com/politics/meet-the-press/poll-nearly-two-thirds-americans-say-social-media-platforms-are-n1266773

**The Pew Research Center study reference above is from "Critical Posts Get More Likes, Comments, and Shares than Other Posts." February 21, 2017. https://www.pewresearch.org/politics/2017/02/23/partisan-conflict-and-congressional-outreach/pdl-02-23-17_antipathy-new-00-02/*

The Humility to Accept Help
SEPTEMBER 21

Last Thursday, I got a sneak peek at Disney World's latest Epcot attraction—Remy's Ratatouille Adventure. The ride doesn't officially open to the public until October 1, but my family and I were invited to an advanced preview.

In short, we loved it!

Based on the Disney/Pixar animated movie *Ratatouille*, the attraction "shrinks" guests down to the size of a rat and then scurries them on a 4D adventure through Gusteau's bustling Parisian restaurant.

If you're not familiar with the movie, the story revolves around an exceptional rat named Remy, who has the "gift of highly developed senses." He can taste and smell what the rest of the rat colony cannot.

Remy dreams of using his unusual talent to become a gourmet chef. When an unexpected encounter with a shotgun-toting homeowner separates Remy from the rest of his colony, he finds himself wandering the backstreets of Paris.

Alone and rain-drenched, Remy eventually makes his way into the kitchen of Gusteau's Restaurant, where he meets Linguini, the bistro's lowly garbage boy. Together, the tandem creates culinary masterpieces.

By hiding under Linguini's hat and guiding the garbage boy's movements like a marionette, Remy helps Linguini gain the praise of a popular food critic. The restaurant thrives because of Remy and Linguini's teamwork.

Riding Remy's Ratatouille Adventure made me think about a commonly overlooked element to the art of being a good teammate: the ability to humble yourself and accept help—for the good of your team.

We typically think of a good teammate as being someone who uses their talents to help the other members of their team. In *Ratatouille*, Remy uses his talents to help his struggling teammate (Linguini) and his team (Gusteau's Restaurant) achieve success. Without question, Remy is a good teammate.

But, in the above example, so is Linguini.

Linguini had to accept Remy's help. He had to set his pride aside, recognize his need for help, and embrace the idea that accepting help was the best way to help his team.

Too many people let their pride keep them from accepting help. They are reluctant to acknowledge their shortcomings and that reluctancy holds them back, which prevents their team from moving forward.

Those people need to be reminded that stubbornness is not a virtue. Humility is. Caring enough about your team to swallow your pride and accept help is the mark of a good teammate and a mindset that leads to efficiency.

Teammates who help others as well as teammates who accept help should be equally revered because they both contribute to team success.

As always…Good teammates care. Good teammates share. Good teammates listen. Go be a good teammate.

Keeping Stress from Becoming Distress
SEPTEMBER 28

Being a part of a team can be one of life's most fulfilling experiences. But it can also be one of life's most frustrating experiences.

As a member of a team, the measure of your achievement is tied to your team's success—something which you, as an individual, do not solely control. Regardless of how hard you work, how greatly you sacrifice, or how spectacularly you perform, your team might still lose.

With teams, success is ultimately dependent on the performance of the entire team—not just that of the individual.

How do you, as a driven individual, keep the stress that comes from this hardened premise from hampering you or your team?

First, don't allow the stress to become distress. At its most elementary level, stress is your body's natural reaction to a situation that challenges your level of comfort. Failure is uncomfortable and can therefore be expected to be accompanied by stress.

Distress is the result of prolonged stress. Distress erodes individual wellbeing, and for teams, it leads to dysfunction.

Good teammates prevent stress from becoming distress by accepting stress's inescapable presence and employing healthy problem-focused coping strategies. They don't waste their energy blaming, shaming, or complaining. They focus on remedying the problem.

Complaining about the team's failures, trying to assign or shift blame, or shaming other team members for their mistakes perpetuates stress. These approaches are not effective ways of holding others accountable. They're ways to keep the stress in the present instead of moving it to the past.

You may not be able to control the team's success, but you can influence it with your effort and enthusiasm—two entities that *are* within your control.

We all have a fire burning inside of us, and we have total control over what we choose to do with that fire. Good teammates use their fire to ignite. Poor teammates use it to inflame.

How hard you work, how greatly you sacrifice, and how spectacularly you perform can ignite your teammates' passions. Your example can inspire them to elevate their effort and enthusiasm, which improves the probability of your team achieving success.

On the other hand, how hard you complain, how greatly you blame, or how unspectacularly you shame can inflame your team with jealousy, pettiness, and resentment. Your negative response to the stress can agitate your fellow teammates and diminish your team's chances of achieving success.

Knowing that you did not allow your stress to become distress and that you controlled what you could control keeps the frustration of being part of team from overtaking the fulfillment of being part of a team.

As always…Good teammates care. Good teammates share. Good teammates listen. Go be a good teammate.

It's Nice to Be Nice
OCTOBER 5

Today is *National Be Nice Day*. Periodically, I check the National Day Calendar to see what special days are coming up. I do this partly for my own amusement (What's more amusing than discovering it's *National Sneak Some Zucchini Into Your Neighbor's Porch Day?*) and partly because sometimes, like today, I happen upon material for a related blog.

The National Day Calendar website usually lists its entries' origins. For instance, *National Sneak Some Zucchini Into Your Neighbor's Porch Day* was started by Tom and Ruth Roy—curators of more than eighty Calendar entries, including such gems as *No Socks Day, Cat Herders' Day,* and *Blah Blah Blah Day.*

The Roys created their zucchini holiday as a way to "donate" their unusually bountiful zucchini harvest to their unsuspecting neighbors.

I wondered how *National Be Nice Day* came to be. Who championed the idea? What event or series of events led to its creation? To my disappointment, the National Day Calendar website provided no details, and despite my quasi-exhaustive research (I clicked through 40+ pages of Google search results), I was unable to unearth a backstory.

This left me to fill in the details with my own unsubstantiated—yet probably right—speculations.

At some point in history, somebody grew so tired of dealing with mean, selfish people that they lost their wits. They then proceeded to scream in a never-witnessed-before manner: "Why can't they just be nice?"

The deeper I dive into the art of being a good teammate, the more probable I find that scenario to be. Dealing with the *un-nice* can be maddening.

Plenty of people think they are nice, but they aren't. Their flawed self-assessment stems from their lack of understanding of the comprehensiveness of the term. The dictionary offers at least eight different meanings of nice (pleasant, agreeable, kind, etc.). The thesaurus provides more than ninety synonyms (cordial, tactful, virtuous, etc.). People mistakenly take a cafeteria approach to the word. They try to pick and choose which meanings they want to apply.

They're pleasant, but they're not necessarily virtuous. They're agreeable, but they're not necessarily tactful. To be nice, all the meanings must apply. (All the meanings are also all attainable!)

Much like being a good teammate, being nice is nothing more than a choice. The question, therefore, isn't so much

"Why can't they be nice?" as it is "Why do they not choose to be nice?"

The answer is fear. They're scared of being taken advantage of. They're scared of being rejected. They're scared of what being nice might cost them (reputation, status, victories, etc.).

I say hogwash to all those objections. They're all byproducts of selfishness.

The great Bear Bryant famously stated, "It costs nothing to be nice." And he was right. It's nice to be nice.

I've written about the undeserving stigma attached to being nice on a previous occasion (*Teammate Tuesdays Volume III*, Chapter 3: "Nice Guys Are the Only Ones Who Finish"). Those scared of the costs of being nice lack vision. They are shortsighted.

Being nice is an investment. Like all great investments, it can take time for the venture to pay dividends. Whether people are nice to you to or not, choose to be nice to them. Because in the end, the investment isn't in others, it's in yourself.

How you treat others—how *nice* you are—will be the measure of your life.

As always…Good teammates care. Good teammates share. Good teammates listen. Go be a good teammate.

*Visit www.wellcat.com and https://.www.nationaltoday.com/national-sneak-zucchini-onto-neighbors-porch-day/ for more details about Tom and Ruth Roy and their holidays.

25

Elevator Teammates
OCTOBER 12

Prior to 1970, only two mega-cities (urban areas with populations exceeding ten million inhabitants) existed in the world—Tokyo and New York City. By 1990, there were ten. Today, there are thirty-four. The United Nations predicts by 2030 that number will swell to forty-three.

While sociologists debate the reasons behind the growth of mega-cities, they generally agree upon what made the growth possible—elevators. Advancements in elevators allowed cities to grow *vertically*.

I was speaking to a group of educators recently who shared with me some of the challenges that are keeping them and their students from growing vertically. Many of their horror stories involved interactions with *helicopter parents* and *lawnmower parents*.

If you're unfamiliar with the terms, they're buzzwords in education. Helicopter parents "hover" over their children. They are overprotective and overinvolved in their children's lives. Lawnmower parents are even more overbearing. They "mow down" obstacles in their children's lives to keep their children from experiencing failure, disappointment, or discomfort.

As I listened to the educators talk, a thought occurred to me: We don't need helicopter or lawnmower parents; we need *elevator parents.*

Elevator parents lift their children with encouragement. But they also smoothly bring their children back down to reality with the understanding that adversity is part of the journey and that failure can be one of life's best teachers.

Helicopter and lawnmower parents hinder their children's development. Though often well-intentioned, their behaviors fuel entitlement and leave their children ill-equipped to handle adversity. They cause their children to grow flat, complacent, and comfortable—instead of *vertically.*

Elevator parents, by comparison, help their children develop the social-emotional skills to be resilient—an attribute of good teammates.

Similar to elevator parents, elevator teammates positively impact the growth and development of their teams. When the team is emotionally down, elevator teammates use their energy to raise morale. When the team is overconfident and sidetracked by the high of temporary success, elevator teammates use their influence to smoothly lower the euphoria and refocus the team on its long-term objectives.

Elevators facilitate the growth of mega-cities. Elevator teammates facilitate the growth of *mega-successful* teams.

Before the introduction of modern elevators, most residential buildings were limited to a few stories. To avoid climbing the stairs and the dangers of fires, wealthier residents chose to live on the lower floors. The poor lived on the higher floors. Elevators reversed that trend. Now, the wealthy enjoy the penthouse views of the top floors, while the poorer residents live on the lower floors.

If your team has stopped growing or is trending in the wrong direction, the introduction of elevator teammates may be the key to reversing your team's fortunes.

As always…Good teammates care. Good teammates share. Good teammates listen. Go be a good teammate.

The data cited above is from the United Nations, Department of Economic and Social Affairs, Population Division (2018). World Urbanization Prospects: The 2018 Revision.

Twenty Ways to Be Coachable
OCTOBER 19

Good teammates are coachable, meaning they can turn input into improved output. Being coachable is among their most cherished attributes and a large part of what makes them good teammates. Here are twenty ways for you to be coachable:

1. **Practice Self-Awareness.** Know your strengths and shortcomings. Don't be susceptible to your blind spots.

2. **Be Open to Constructive Criticism.** Don't let your ego keep you from hearing what you may not want to hear.

3. **Don't Take Criticism Personally.** Think about why it's said and not how it's said.

4. **Crave Feedback.** Purposefully solicit wide-ranging assessments.

5. **Have a Desire to Please and Exceed Expectations.** Find out what is desired from you and not just by you.

6. **Want to Be Held Accountable.** Don't get defensive or make excuses for falling short of expectations.

7. **Be Willing to Abandon Your Comfort Zone.** Personal growth happens beyond the confines of personal comfort.

8. **Exercise Humility.** Value others' opinions without indulging in self-righteousness.

9. **Listen with Your Ears and Your Eyes.** Look speakers in the eye when they're talking.

10. **Listen with Intent.** Digest the meaning of what is said before responding.

11. **Affirm Instructions.** Nod your head and let the speaker know you understand what you're being told.

12. **Provide Feedback.** Give your "coach" insights into what you're experiencing so that they can best help you.

13. **Adopt an Unwavering Commitment.** Be "all in" and fully devoted to getting better.

14. **Be Keen to Try New Approaches.** What worked in the past might not work in the future.

15. **Apply the Instructions You've Been Given.** Don't only accept the feedback, apply it.

16. **Practice Positive Body Language.** No eye rolling! No slouching shoulders! No shaking heads!

17. **Be Process Driven.** Work independently without modifying or skipping steps.

18. **Squelch Arrogant Tendencies.** Accept that your way may not be the best way.

19. **Have Long-Term Vision.** Be easy to please, but hard to satisfy, by staying focused on long-term goals instead of short-term gains.

20. **Be Grateful.** Appreciate that someone cares enough about you to share their observations and suggestions.

I have yet to meet an individual who brings value to their team who does not value the opportunity to get better—*for their team*. When the individual improves, the team improves. Improvement starts with being coachable.

As always…Good teammates care. Good teammates share. Good teammates listen. Go be a good teammate.

The Curse of Revenge
OCTOBER 26

Halloween week brings an abundance of jack-o-lanterns, costumes, trick-or-treating, and of course horror films. Check the television listings this week and you will discover plentiful airings of *Friday the 13th*, *Halloween*, *A Nightmare on Elm Street*, and countless other scary movies.

Have you ever noticed how the psychopathic behaviors of villains in classic horror films are always initially motivated by revenge?

Jason Voorhees (*Friday the 13th*) sought revenge on the teenager who killed his mother—who herself sought revenge on the irresponsible Camp Crystal Lake counselors she blamed for her son's drowning.

Michael Myers (*Halloween*) was bullied by a classmate and his mother's abusive boyfriend before going on his terror spree. Freddie Krueger (*A Nightmare on Elm Street*) was burned to death by a group of vigilantes before haunting his victims' dreams.

Revenge may make a good motive for a horror movie villain but not so much for a good teammate. Wanting to get back at someone who wronged you is understandable. The idea of inflicting hurt on the person or persons responsible for hurting you can be rather appealing. But psychologically, it can also be rather damaging—and wasteful.

A few years ago, scientists from the University of Geneva (Switzerland) studied the brain activity of participants who were wronged in an experiment and subsequently given the opportunity to exact revenge on those who had cheated them.

The scientists observed an immediate boost in neurological activity in the area of the participants' brains associated with rewards. However, they also found that activity to be short lived, producing similar results as cocaine and nicotine use. As it turns out, revenge does not keep rewarding.

In fact, the opposite happens. We expect revenge to be cathartic. We expect it to provide closure and free us from our emotional baggage. But it actually aggravates our wounds by prolonging the hurt of the original offense. Revenge is a curse because it leads to vindictive and malicious decisions.

Our inability to "let it go" and heal becomes a form of self-punishment, making us as grotesque on the inside as Jason Voorhees, Michael Myers, and Freddy Krueger are on the outside.

Good teammates realize that exacting revenge requires energy. While the possibility of punishing a perpetrator can be enticing, they know they are better served by asserting their energy elsewhere.

The next time you think about wasting your time on revenge, I hope Jason Voorhees' "ki-ki-ki-ma-ma-ma" leitmotif from *Friday the 13th* enters your head and that it serves as a reminder to assert your energy elsewhere.

As always…Good teammates care. Good teammates share. Good teammates listen. Go be a good teammate.

The University of Geneva study referenced above is from Jaffe, Eric. "The Complicated Psychology of Revenge." The Association of Psychological Science, May 4, 2011. www.psychologicalscience.org/observer/the-complicated-psychology-of-revenge

Oxygen Mask Omissions
NOVEMBER 2

As a frequent flyer, I've watched flight attendants give the pre-flight "oxygen mask" presentation a thousand times.

> *In the event of a sudden loss in cabin pressure, oxygen masks will drop from the overhead compartments. Place the mask over your mouth and nose. Pull the strings to tighten the mask. Be sure to secure your mask before attempting to help others.*

The last part of that message about securing your mask before attempting to help others has become a trendy analogy for the importance of practicing self-care. How can you help others if you are yourself physically or emotionally incapacitated?

At high altitudes, a loss in cabin pressure causes hypoxia—where the body shuts down from a lack of oxygen. Without sufficient oxygen, passengers lose consciousness. You can't help another passenger, like a child, put on their oxygen mask if you are unconscious. The oxygen mask/self-care analogy makes sense.

However, I fear as society continues to (rightfully) emphasize the importance of self-care, a crucial component of that analogy is slipping away. Like a lot of passengers, I've been guilty of not giving the pre-flight instructions my full attention. After a while, I start to tune out.

In the event of a sudden loss in cabin pressure, oxygen masks will drop from the overhead compartments. Place the mask over your mouth and nose...blah, blah, blah.

Unfortunately, the same is happening to the oxygen mask analogy. People are getting the part about putting on their mask first (self-care) but omitting the reason why they are putting their mask on first.

The oxygen mask analogy is turning into "you do you" and "me first."

What comes after the "..." is crucial because the rest of the message provides context to the motive. You are putting your mask on first so that you can help those who cannot help themselves put on their mask. The purpose of your action is team-driven, not self-driven. Without purpose beyond self, the concept of self-care is just repackaged selfishness.

To be clear, not taking care oneself, not getting enough rest, not recharging one's batteries, or allowing oneself to burnout are equally selfish.

Good teammates embrace the value of self-care, as well as the purpose for it. They appreciate that self-care can help them become more efficient and make them more sustainable. They care enough to care for themselves—so that they can best care for the needs of their team. And they encourage other members of their team to do the same.

As always…Good teammates care. Good teammates share. Good teammates listen. Go be a good teammate.

29

An Opportunity to Teach Empathy
NOVEMBER 9

One of the most challenging aspects of writing *Teammate Tuesdays* is delivering content that is relevant to a diverse following of teams. People from human resources, corporate sales teams, corporate management teams, church organizations, nonprofits, school administrations, faculty teams, and sports teams all read it.

Though structurally different, every one of those teams has something in common: They're all looking for ways to improve teamwork by improving the mindset of their individual teammates.

I do my best to share content that is ambiguous enough to apply to all teams. Today's topic is directed specifically at scholastic sports coaches, but the message should resonate with every team because the issue impacts everyone.

Last week, a California high school football team defeated its opponent 106-0. The team scored 56 points in the first quarter and was up 83-0 at half time. Their quarterback threw for 13 touchdowns during the game.

In what was perhaps the game's most contentious play, the coach elected to go for a two-point conversion despite already leading 104-0.

As would be expected, the lopsided victory drew plenty of disapproval. Legendary sportscaster Dick Vitale tweeted: "How can the Coaching staff…feel good about themselves?…U SHOULD BE FIRED!"

Whenever I hear stories like this, I can't help but think of the famous Winston Churchill quote: Those that fail to learn from history are doomed to repeat it.

Not that long ago, the world was outraged by the Texas girls basketball team who beat their opponent 100-0. The coach of that team was fired shortly thereafter for refusing to apologize for running up the score, telling the *Dallas Morning News*, "(M)y girls played with honor and integrity."

Maybe they did. But their coaches did not. Running up the score is an egregious, indefensible act for a coach.

The principal of the California high school football team responsible for last week's egregiousness subsequently released an apology for the team's lack of sportsmanship.

Condemning the lack of sportsmanship is reasonable. However, some would argue that players lowering their standards and not competing to their highest level is disrespectful to their competition and equally unsportsmanlike.

For the record, I happen to agree that the coach should be fired in this situation, but not necessarily for his lack of sportsmanship. The coach should be fired for his dereliction of duties.

Scholastic sports should first and foremost be used as a vehicle to teach life lessons. The coach failed miserably in this regard because he missed out on an ideal opportunity to teach empathy—a core component of being a good teammate.

Players who are taught that running up the score is acceptable grow up to be uncompassionate landlords who won't give down-on-their-luck tenants some leeway with overdue rent, uncompassionate bosses who won't cut grieving employees some slack with their workload, and uncompassionate voters who won't consider issues that may not directly affect them.

When society condones running up the score in scholastic sports, we condemn our future. Society needs more empathy and we mustn't squander opportunities to teach this important skill to our youngest members.

Empathy prevents offenses that happen to someone today from happening to someone else tomorrow. Empathy leads to understanding and improved relationships.

As always…Good teammates care. Good teammates share. Good teammates listen. Go be a good teammate.

The Humility and Brevity Address
NOVEMBER 16

Seven score and eighteen years ago this week, Abraham Lincoln delivered one of the most iconic speeches in American history. If your nineteenth century math is a little rusty, that's one hundred and fifty-eight years ago. And if your U.S. history is a little rusty, the iconic speech was the Gettysburg Address.

On the afternoon of November 19, 1863, a crowd gathered for the dedication of the Gettysburg National Cemetery. The ceremony was held on the battlefield where Union forces had defeated the Confederates some four and a half months prior.

Most don't realize that Lincoln's speech, though now commonly known as the "Gettysburg Address," wasn't the real Gettysburg Address.

The keynote address that day was actually given by a dignitary named Edward Everett, who was widely recognized as the period's most popular and respected orator. Everett spoke for over two hours—customary practice and the expected length in that era for that type of speech.

Lincoln was asked to make a few remarks after Everett had finished. Lincoln's brief, two-minute remarks became what is most remembered about the occasion.

Everett later wrote to Lincoln, humbly stating that the President had accomplished in two minutes what he had tried to do in two hours. As Lincoln's words went that generation's equivalent of viral, Everett recognized that their impact exceeded that of his much longer speech—and he wasn't too proud to acknowledge that fact.

The appropriateness of Everett's response highlights two important aspects of being a good teammate: humility and brevity.

Good teammates are never jealous of their fellow teammates' success. If another team member outperforms them, they possess the humility to acknowledge and appreciate the better performance. They refuse to be jealous or resentful.

Their response is an indication of their love for their team and a sign of class.

Brevity conveys respect. Good teammates respect others' time. They don't speak any longer than necessary, nor do they speak any shorter than necessary. They communicate precisely, efficiently, and effectively.

Sharing their thoughts in this manner keeps them from rambling, babbling, or talking in circles—all of which unnecessarily rob the listener of valued time.

Humility and brevity are borne of self-awareness. To be a good teammate, you need to be aware of how your words and actions affect others.

While Lincoln's words continue to echo through history, a few from Everett's address are also deserving of that honor.

Everett provided a chronological account of the Gettysburg battle in his speech. When describing the Union's victory, despite the Confederates having "superiority of numbers" and the advantage of choosing the battle's time and place, Everett said: "Victory does not always fall to those who deserve it."

His words are as true today as they were seven score and eighteen years ago. Teams comprised of good teammates have a knack for being victorious, even when they seem to be at a disadvantage.

As always…Good teammates care. Good teammates share. Good teammates listen. Go be a good teammate.

Ten Blessings You Should Be Thankful For
NOVEMBER 23

Last week, I wrote about Abraham Lincoln and the anniversary of the Gettysburg Address. As Americans prepare to celebrate Thanksgiving, it's worth noting another fun fact about Lincoln: He's the one responsible for making Thanksgiving an official national holiday.

A month prior to giving his Gettysburg Address, Lincoln gave a speech declaring that the fourth Thursday in November would from that date forward be considered an official day of thanksgiving (lowercase) in the United States.

While Thanksgiving is typically thought of as honoring the harvest meal between the Pilgrims and Native Americans, Lincoln's declaration came as an expression of gratitude and a way of honoring the Union army's victory at Gettysburg—something he felt the country should be thankful for.

We often use Thanksgiving as an occasion to recognize the blessings for which we are thankful. When you're part of a team, there are certain overlooked blessing for which you should be thankful, including:

1. Someone holding you accountable

2. Having a role to play on your team

3. An opportunity to selflessly use your talents for the greater good

4. Being a part of something bigger than yourself

5. Experiencing fulfillment

6. A chance to invest in others

7. Someone recognizing your contributions

8. Fighting for something you believe in

9. The joy of making shared memories

10. Discovering the courage to overcome challenges

If the above are present in your life, consider yourself blessed. If they are not, consider why they are not. Maybe acquiring them requires a change in your attitude or a change in your approach. Either way, be thankful that both of those options are always at your disposal. From our team to yours, Happy Thanksgiving!

As always…Good teammates care. Good teammates share. Good teammates listen. Go be a good teammate.

32

Giving Forgiveness
NOVEMBER 30

#GivingTuesday always coincides with the weekly release of *Teammate Tuesdays*. And yes, adding the hashtag and mashing the words together (capital "G" and capital "T") is the preferred way to reference the occasion.

I've previously written about the history of #GivingTuesday (*Teammate Tuesdays Volume II*, Chapter 31: "Giving Leads to Inspiration"), so I won't rehash the entire story. The condensed version is that a group of caring individuals in New York City came together in 2012 to create a day that "encourages people to do good."

Now mentioned in the same breath as Black Friday and Cyber Monday, #GivingTuesday (the Tuesday after Thanksgiving) has become a holiday where, according to the organizer's website, hundreds of millions of people "give, collaborate, and celebrate generosity."

When we think about all the ways to be generous and all that can be given, sometimes we look past an incredibly impactful option—forgiveness. Giving forgiveness is a great way to do good, especially for members of a team.

Letting go of feelings of resentment, anger, or vengeance brought on by transgressions releases us from the emotional burden of living in the past. When you forgive, you focus on what happens from that moment forward. The past disappears and becomes inconsequential to you.

For some, giving forgiveness can be hard to do— unthinkable, even. People will try to ease into the process with the approach of *forgiving but not forgetting*. Unfortunately, this flawed approach doesn't bear the fruits of genuine forgiveness.

Forgiving but not forgetting falls into the same category as *trust but verify*. (If you need to verify, it's not trust! It's rhetoric.)

To have genuine trust, you must have faith. To give genuine forgiveness, you must forget. Forgiving and forgetting are inseparable.

When a creditor forgives a debt, whatever was owed is forgotten. The balance due reads zeros. The slate is wiped clean. Banks don't send debtors letters notifying them of their debt being forgiven, then turnaround and send a follow up letter reminding them that they still owe a debt.

Once the debt is forgiven, it disappears. The same applies to forgiving transgressions. Move the transgression to the past and forget about it.

The person who did you harm might not be willing to apologize. They might not feel sorry for their transgressions. They might not deserve forgiveness. The harm they caused might not be worthy of forgetting. But the good that comes from forgiving and forgetting doesn't have to be exclusively viewed from the transgressor's perspective.

Forgiving brings an inner peace to the forgiver that helps them move forward. If someone on your team has harmed you, forgiving their transgressions can lighten your emotional load and free you to focus your energy on more meaningful and productive tasks. Whereas holding onto the harm can weigh you down and turn you into the more toxic teammate.

This #GivingTuesday, consider giving the gift of forgiveness to your transgressors, bearing in mind that often the transgressor most deserving of forgiveness is yourself. Forgive. Forget. Move forward.

As always…Good teammates care. Good teammates share. Good teammates listen. Go be a good teammate.

33

Armadillo Teammates
DECEMBER 7

For the past several weeks, I have been tormented by a menacing armadillo. (In full disclosure, that is a sentence that I never imagined myself writing!) I moved to central Florida a few years ago, but I grew up in western Pennsylvania. We didn't have armadillos in Pennsylvania. There were plenty of opossums, raccoons, and groundhogs, but no armadillos.

Until recently, I naively thought armadillos were exclusive to the southwestern United States. I had only seen them in cowboy movies and zoos. To my surprise, Florida has armadillos too.

Armadillos can be a nuisance. They wreak havoc on lawns and destroy landscaping. Even worse, they burrow under houses and weaken foundations. My armadillo was causing all those issues.

Underperforming teams can be tormented by menaces with similar characteristics to armadillos. I like to refer to these menacing individuals as armadillo teammates.

Hard on the outside, soft on the inside. Armadillos are the only mammals with hard, protective shells. Beneath that shell, however, they are weak and vulnerable. They don't have the necessary combat skills to counter threats. Their shells are their only defense.

Armadillo teammates also have a hard exterior. They aren't warm or welcoming. They come across as disinterested and try to pass themselves off as being tough. But beneath that facade, they are insecure, shallow, and mentally weak. Their hard exterior keeps other team members from getting emotionally close and prevents them from bonding with the rest of the team.

Not blind, but poor vision. Contrary to common belief, armadillos are not blind. But they do have notoriously poor peripheral vision. They struggle to see what is not directly in front of their nose.

Armadillo teammates struggle to see how their actions affect others. They're too focused on themselves to realize the negative impact that comes from their lacking self-awareness.

Hide during the light, do damage in the dark. Armadillos are primarily nocturnal. Their poor vision and anti-social tendencies lead them to be most active after sunset. That means the bulk of the damage they cause is done in the dark.

Armadillo teammates tend to not be confrontational in front of the entire team. They don't speak up when they could or arguably should. They prefer to gossip and complain out of earshot of the team's leadership. Essentially, they also do the bulk of their damage in the dark.

Apart from terminating armadillos, the two best ways to get rid of them are to eliminate their food source and make the environment they've invaded unappealing. That means treating your yard for insects (armadillos' favorite food) and spreading repellents like cayenne pepper or garlic around your yard (armadillos are repulsed by those smells).

As you've probably already guessed, the same strategies apply to ridding your team of armadillo teammates.

Armadillo teammates feast on negativity. You eliminate their "food source" when you kill negativity on your team. Don't give their toxicity an audience. Let their gossip and petty complaints fall on deaf ears.

You can create an "unappealing environment" by building a positive team culture that shuns selfishness and rewards selflessness. Armadillo teammates will feel compelled to either change their habits to assimilate or move on to an environment they find more suiting (i.e. another team).

When teams eliminate members who lack internal fortitude, self-awareness, and the willingness to be transparent in their actions, they begin to flourish—the same way that lawns do once menacing varmints go away.

As always…Good teammates care. Good teammates share. Good teammates listen. Go be a good teammate.

Assimilating Individuality
DECEMBER 14

By now, most of the northern hemisphere has experienced their first snow fall of the season, despite winter not officially arriving until next week. If you're able to get beyond the unpleasantness of the accompanying cold temperatures, the inconvenience of having to clear pathways, and the inevitable disruption to travel plans, falling snow can be an inspiring sight.

Each snowflake is uniquely constructed. No two are ever alike. The real beauty, however, is found in their collective appearance. Snowflakes fall with the harmonious rhythm of a perfectly synched orchestra. The sight is majestic, if not mesmerizing.

I heard a story recently about a Rabbi named Schultz, who bought his friend, Reverend Brown, a Christmas tree ornament from Ahmad, the corner store clerk. On the bottom of the ornament was a sticker that read: Made in India.

To summarize, the ornament was made by a Hindu, sold by a Muslim, gifted by a Jew to a Christian. If you're able to get beyond the marginally offensive stereotypes, the story offers an inspiring insight about maintaining identity and purpose.

One of the most difficult aspects of being part of a team is finding a way to assimilate into the team's culture without abandoning your individuality. Some refuse to believe that to be possible. Others believe the answer lies in replacing standardization with inclusion.

Maybe. But that's more of a big picture leadership strategy that isn't necessarily within any individual member's control. You may not be able to dictate policy change on that level. So what can *you* do as an individual to influence your approach to this issue?

First, learn to embrace the value of diversity. See different perspectives as assets that contribute to your team's beauty the same way that different snowflakes contribute to the beauty of a snowfall. Just remember, though differently shaped, every snowflake falls in the same direction.

Regardless of whatever individuality you seek to preserve, you must maintain a commitment to working toward a common team objective that overrides any individual agendas.

Second, choose to prioritize your purpose over your differences. Maintaining a commitment to a common team objective requires an adherence to several universally respected values—determination, compassion, integrity, etc.

Once you accept your commitment to those values as being your most significant identifier, all other identifiers become immaterial.

None of the individuals in the above story needed to abandon their individuality to play their part in the life cycle of the Christmas tree ornament because they shared a commitment to purpose. Rabbi Schultz gifted with kindness. Reverend Brown accepted with gratitude. Ahmad sold with friendliness. And the unnamed Hindu presumedly manufactured with diligence.

When your commitment to service and purpose becomes your primary identity, you transcend the issue of assimilation.

By the way, the story of Rabbi Schultz and Reverend Brown ends with both friends smiling—a universal expression of happiness. Service leads to purpose. Purpose leads to happiness.

As always...Good teammates care. Good teammates share. Good teammates listen. Go be a good teammate.

Ten Reasons Why the Elf on the Shelf Is a Good Teammate
DECEMBER 21

Do you have an Elf on the Shelf in your home? They bring joy to millions of families (teams!) every year. Here are ten reasons why the Elf on the Shelf is a good teammate:

1. **They help us hold ourselves accountable.** We think twice before we act because we know our elves are always watching.

2. **They are egoless.** Our elves happily accept whatever name we give them. They are more concerned with doing their job than their title.

3. **They show up when they are most needed.** The holidays can be stressful, and our elves always seem to appear in our homes at just the right time.

4. **They take their role seriously.** Our elves never move, speak, or abandon their post in the presence of children—exactly the way the Santa instructed.

5. **They recognize, share, and praise others' good teammate moves.** Our elves report our positive actions back to Santa without resentment or jealousy.

6. **They are faithful.** Our elves remain diligent throughout the day and they return ever morning like clockwork. We can always count on them.

7. **They inspire creativity on their team.** We never know where our elves will pop up or in what antics we'll discover them to have been involved.

8. **They provide levity.** Occasionally, the team needs a little comic relief to reduce the tension. Our elves' shenanigans provide us with well-timed laughs.

9. **They practice self-awareness.** Our elves never overstay their welcome. When the Christmas season ends, they know their job is done. They return home to the North Pole without incident or fanfare.

10. **They connect the team.** Our elves are a bonding experience. Their presence provides us with cherished memories.

As always…Good teammates care. Good teammates share. Good teammates listen. Go be a good teammate.

The Year in Review
DECEMBER 28

We've been fortunate to build a loyal following on social media and have seen that following grow again this year. Our "teammates" enjoy the inspirational thoughts we post each day, and we enjoy sharing the message.

Many followers have found our daily posts to be an opportunity to refuel their good teammate tanks, rediscover purpose in their lives, and refocus their energies. In keeping with our annual *Teammate Tuesday* tradition, here are the posts from each of the past twelve months that received the most interactions, impressions, shares, likes, favorites, and retweets:

JANUARY

"For anyone who's part of a team, remember: Good teammates are never stingy with compliments."

FEBRUARY

"The 4 'E's' that determine how good of a teammate you are: 1. Effort 2. Energy 3. Enthusiasm 4. Empathy."

MARCH

"A productive team culture is not a coincidence, it's the result of a choice. The individual members of that team chose to be good teammates and put the teams' needs ahead of their own. WE>me."

APRIL

"'When life gives you lemons…' (*Sometimes the only thing keeping lemons from becoming lemonade is your attitude. Don't allow something you can control to be your biggest obstacle.)"

MAY

"The first step to building a good team is building good teammates. Focus on molding the individual members' habits/mindsets and team success will take care of itself."

JUNE

"Drama, complaining, and gossip pollute teams. Good teammates don't create pollution, they come up with solutions."

JULY

"Choose to be a contributor, not a depleter or hindrance. Good teammates are consumed with production, not obstruction."

AUGUST

"WE is always greater than ME. But WE starts with ME choosing to be a good teammate. A team with good teammates can overcome any obstacle."

SEPTEMBER

"Good teammates ignite. (passion, inspiration, love...) Bad teammates inflame (jealousy, pettiness, resentment...)."

OCTOBER

"If you want to build good teammates, you must get team members to understand this fact: Admitting your mistakes is not a sign of weakness. It's a sign of awareness and an indication of humility. It's the start of growth."

NOVEMBER

"Good teammates don't form teams of their own. In other words: NO CLIQUES! Cliques are mini teams within the main team that destroy the main team from the inside out. Avoid them at all costs!"

DECEMBER

"A big part of being a good teammate is knowing the difference between what you can control and what you cannot control. Good teammates must be masters of their attitudes. You may not be able to control the trigger event, but you can control how you handle it."

We hope you will continue to support our Good Teammate efforts, as we strive to reach a larger audience and inspire even more individuals to become better teammates. Simply put, the world cannot have too many good teammates.

If you know of someone who could benefit from a dose of the Good Teammate message, please encourage them to join the conversation and start following us on social media. They can connect with us on the following sites:

Facebook: *https://www.facebook.com/coachloya*
Twitter: *https://twitter.com/coachlanceloya*
Instagram: *https://www.instagram.com/lanceloya*
LinkedIn: *https://www.linkedin.com/in/coachloya*

As always...Good teammates care. Good teammates share. Good teammates listen. Go be a good teammate.

Countering Shallow Ambition
JANUARY 4

At some point in every team leader's life they will be approached by a seemingly ambitious member of the team and asked: *What can I do to get _____?*

For sports coaches, the blank is usually filled in with "more playing time." For teachers, it's usually "a better grade." And for bosses, it's usually some variation of "a promotion."

Being approached with this question can be invigorating for leaders. You're moved by the person's ambition, so you provide them with encouragement and a list of improvements they need to make. For example:

Player: *What can I do to get more playing time?*

Coach: *You need to work on your shooting. If you can prove yourself to be a more consistent shooter, you'll definitely earn more playing time.*

The person inevitably thanks you when you're finished and offers an assurance to commit to the suggested improvements. Unfortunately, that conversation turns out to be the depth of their commitment. A few days or weeks pass, and the person approaches you again with the exact same question: *What can I do to get* _____ *?*

It becomes a recurring interaction: They ask what they can do to get more. You tell them. But they don't follow through with your suggestions. What was initially invigorating is now exhausting. You realize the shallowness of their ambition.

They want the perks, without paying the price. Their strategy for getting "more" wasn't to make a deeper commitment; it was to get your attention and nag you into giving them what they had not earned.

How can a team leader handle this situation without hurting their team? Consider flipping the script. While nagging is not generally an effective strategy for growth, nagging can be an effective method for countering shallow ambition and creating empathy.

Be extra thorough with your suggestions for how the person can get what they seek. Provide them with detailed, measurable instructions that cannot be misinterpreted and then be relentless in monitoring their efforts.

Every time you see you them, inquire about their progress. *Did you work on your shooting today? How many shots did you shoot today? What shooting drills did you do today? How many shots are you going to shoot tomorrow? How much did you improve?*

Your relentless monitoring—your investment in them—will lead to them diving deeper into their commitment or relinquishing their previous strategy. Either way, the team will benefit from their change.

As always…Good teammates care. Good teammates share. Good teammates listen. Go be a good teammate.

The Burnt Ends Perspective
JANUARY 11

If you're a regular *Teammate Tuesday* reader, you're likely aware of my fondness for barbeque. I've written previously about the "good teammate" lessons gained from my barbeque adventures (*Teammate Tuesdays Volume II*, Chapter 3: "Ellie Lou's Secret").

Last week, I was at a convention in Kansas City—a place many consider to be the mecca of the barbeque world. Kansas City is home to more than one hundred mouth-watering barbeque joints. Their prominence is rooted in the city's historical connection to the stockyards and meatpacking industry. Pitmasters have been perfecting their barbeque recipes in Kansas City since the early 1920s.

After the Kansas City Chiefs won Super Bowl LIV, head coach Andy Reid (a renowned barbeque connoisseur) mentioned in a post-game interview that he was looking forward to going home and eating some "burnt ends"—a local delicacy.

Burnt ends are the trimmed edges of brisket. When brisket is smoked, the fatty pieces around the outer edge tend to dry out and develop a hardened, bark-like texture.

Pitmasters used to discard these charred edges— mistakenly assuming that nobody would want to eat them. One day a Kansas City pitmaster named Arthur Bryant started handing out "burnt ends" as a snack to customers waiting on their orders.

Bryant's customers fell in love with the intense smoky flavor. Burnt ends were a big hit and it wasn't long before they became a staple of every barbeque joint in Kansas City. What were formerly thought of as worthless scraps have been transformed into the measure of quality barbeque.

Ever since watching that Andy Reid interview, I have been wanting to try real Kansas City burnt ends. I finally got the chance to do so last week, and they did not disappoint!

I ate burnt ends at the original Joe's Kansas City BBQ (a spot holder on Anthony Bourdain's list of "13 Places to Eat Before You Die"). I ate burnt ends at Fiorella's Jack Stack Barbecue (Andy Reid's favorite barbeque spot). I ate burnt ends at Q39 (the place where Andy Reid dined immediately after winning Super Bowl LIV). I even ate them at a restaurant called Burnt End BBQ!

The offerings at each were every bit as delicious as I anticipated.

So where's the "good teammate" lesson in this story? Sometimes we mistakenly assume team members to not be of value to the team because we view them from a misguided perspective. We gauge their merits based solely on traditional benchmarks instead of the potential advantage their uniqueness offers. Before discarding them, it's important to consider what's behind our false assessments.

Maybe they've been placed in the wrong position or assigned the wrong role. Maybe the team isn't tapping into their true talents. Maybe the team needs to alter its strategies around their talents, instead of expecting it to be the other way around. A simple adjustment can lead to a dramatic difference in how these team members are perceived.

Like burnt ends, all some teammates need to be transformed into a bigger contributor is an opportunity to showcase their merits from a different perspective. Providing them with that opportunity is a good teammate move worth pursuing—and one that will also not disappoint.

As always...Good teammates care. Good teammates share. Good teammates listen. Go be a good teammate.

The Andy Reid interview referenced above is from Thorman, Joel. "Breaking: Andy Reid's Favorite KC Barbecue Revealed." SB Nation, July 25, 2013. https://www.arrowheadpride.com/2013/7/25/4558478/andy-reid-barbecue-kansas-city-jack-stack

Five Rules for Pursuing Individual Goals While Still Being a Good Teammate
JANUARY 18

No successful team leaders have ever wished for the members of their team to just be content with where they are. Successful team leaders despise complacency. They want team members who are driven to level up.

Although it may seem contrary to popular belief, pursuing individual goals while still being a good teammate is possible—provided you follow several important rules. Here are five of them:

1. **Set Individual Goals That Advance Team Goals.** If the team's goal is to win a championship, then improving your individual skills, technique, or knowledge can help your team reach its overarching goal. Developing and then committing to a plan to improve your individual skills (e.g. A softball player

who spends an extra hour each day hitting in the batting cage) will make the team better, because: *When the individual improves, the team improves.*

2. **Don't Compromise Team Goals for Individual Goals.** Your individual goals cannot conflict with the team's goals. Setting individual goals tied to specific statistics can be counterproductive. For instance, a quarterback sets an individual goal of passing for 200 yards in a game. Going into the fourth quarter, the quarterback has accumulated 160 yards. But his team is holding onto a lead and the weather has changed to no longer be conducive to passing the ball. It's in the team's best interest to hand the ball off and run out the clock. For the quarterback to continue to pursue his individual statistical goal would be selfish and potentially undermine his team's goal of winning the game.

3. **Don't Use Team Time for Individual Goals.** Working on individual goals during team time is not a wise decision. Respect the difference between team time and personal time. In the above example of the softball player, spending an extra hour hitting balls in the batting cage is a commendable use of that player's time. But not so much if that player were to be hitting balls in the batting cage when she was supposed to be working on infield practice or watching film with the rest of the team. Using team time for individual development opens you up to

having your intentions misconstrued. You risk being mistaken as selfish and only "in it" for yourself.

4. **Share Your Goals with Others.** Make the other members of your team aware of your individual goals. Sharing those details may inspire them to become similarly driven. As humans, we have a natural desire to help others. By openly sharing your individual goals, you also make it possible for your teammates to become invested in you. Their encouragement can get you through challenging times and assist you in holding yourself accountable.

5. **Don't Let Your Passion Displace Your Purpose.** It's great to be passionate about your individual goals but stay true to the purpose for having them: To help your team succeed. When outsiders start to notice the fruits of your labor, the attention may prompt you to be more focused on individual accolades than team achievement. Refuse to give into this temptation. Remain humble, loyal, and grateful to your team and your fellow teammates.

As always...Good teammates care. Good teammates share. Good teammates listen. Go be a good teammate

Good Teammates Rise Up
JANUARY 25

After several missed opportunities and unfortunate postponements, I was finally able to see *Hamilton* on Broadway. I had been wanting to see the New York City production for quite some time and can now say with confidence that it was worth waiting for.

Hamilton lived up to the hype—and then some!

I considered dedicating this week's blog to discussing the issue of whether Alexander Hamilton, Aaron Burr, Thomas Jefferson, or any of the other founding fathers featured in the musical were good teammates. However, I've decided against doing so.

To truly understand that issue requires a certain degree of familiarity with the musical—something I suspect not all *Teammate Tuesday* readers possess. For that reason, I'm going to instead focus on an inspiring "good teammate" lesson derived from the show's origins.

In 2009, a young Lin-Manuel Miranda, the show's creator, was invited to perform before President Barrack Obama at the White House Poetry Jam. Miranda told the audience that he was going to do a song from a hip hop album he was working on about the life of former Secretary of Treasury Alexander Hamilton, a person he thought "embodies hip hop." The audience laughed at the absurdity of Miranda's assertion.

President Obama would later recall that after Miranda told him he was going to do a "rap about Alexander Hamilton," the president snarked: "Well, good luck with that."

Receiving that sort of discouraging response could have derailed Miranda. But much like his musical's namesake, Miranda remained young, scrappy, and hungry—and committed. He didn't throw away his shot. He forged ahead with determination.

Six years later, *Hamilton* would make its theatrical debut on Broadway. The rest is, as they say, history. (In this case, literally!) *Hamilton* has become one of the most successful musicals of all time.

By remaining committed to his convictions, Miranda facilitated *Hamilton's* success. Moreover, his determination led to a number of noteworthy "good teammate moves," including:

- Sharing his knowledge in a creative and memorable way. (Miranda was moved to write the musical after reading Ron Chernow's biography, *Alexander Hamilton*.)

- Inspiring enthusiasm for American history. (My daughter correctly answered a question on her civics exam because she remembered a lyric from a *Hamilton* song about the Battle of Yorktown.)

- Embracing tradition while additionally incorporating progressiveness with regard to race and gender. (Many of the roles in *Hamilton* are cast outside of their traditional stereotypes.)

Good teammates do all the above. They routinely share their knowledge, inspire enthusiasm, embrace tradition and progressiveness, and they remain committed to their convictions. That commitment is what sees their teams through tough times and allows them to *rise up*.

As always…Good teammates care. Good teammates share. Good teammates listen. Go be a good teammate.

*Barack O'Bama's comments in the interview referenced above can be viewed at https://www.youtube.com/watch?v=BchNer_kfB8&t=8s

Dismissive and Defensive
FEBRUARY 1

Of the many admirable qualities of good teammates, how they handle criticism is among their most impressive. Good teammates have an incredible ability to resist being dismissive or defensive.

Being dismissive means interpreting the criticism as unworthy of your consideration. You reject what is being said with an attitude of superiority. A dismissive response reeks of arrogance and self-righteousness. *It's preposterous to think that could be true of my actions.*

Being defensive means interpreting the criticism as unmerited. You blame someone or something else for your missteps. You make excuses. A defensive response reeks of insecurity and deficient self-awareness. *It's not my fault. That's how I was told to do it. So and so did it the same way.*

A lot of people default to one of these two responses when provided with negative feedback. Being dismissive or defensive is instinctive and even understandable—and quite possibly justified. The critic may be too unfamiliar with the situation or unqualified to be judging your actions. Legitimate reasons for your behavior may exist. Your excuses may be valid.

But none of that matters to good teammates. They refuse to respond to criticism dismissively or defensively because they crave feedback.

Good teammates are committed to becoming the best possible versions of themselves. For that to happen, they need others to help them see their blind spots. Responding dismissively or defensively to criticism will make others reluctant to voice their assessments.

This does not mean that good teammates automatically accept the authority of the critic nor the merits of the critique. It simply means that they have the confidence and humility to listen to feedback.

Good teammates know you learn by listening, not speaking. Instead of being dismissive or defensive, good teammates digest and discern. They don't take the criticism personally. They listen intently without interrupting, mull over what was said, and then consider how the information can be applied to their life.

To effectively digest and discern, they must sometimes move beyond what was said and who it was said by and reflect on why it was said. Perhaps the critic has ill-intentions, or perhaps the critic is perceiving your actions in a way that you are unaware.

If the latter is the case, you need to be cognizant of the concept of perception being reality and commit to changing that perception.

The idea of not listening to criticism from someone whom you would not take advice has become trendy in leadership circles. But this can be a dangerous philosophy for team leaders to embrace.

Just as a good leader knows that a valuable idea can come from anyone, a good teammate knows that a valid critique can also come from anyone. Good teammates are wise enough, humble enough, and courageous enough to embrace this premise.

The next time someone criticizes you, politely thank them for sharing their thoughts. Digest what was said. Consider why it was said. And find a way to use the experience to help you become a better teammate.

As always…Good teammates care. Good teammates share. Good teammates listen. Go be a good teammate.

Ten Ways to Show Love to Your Teammates
FEBRUARY 8

Love is a complex entity. Its meaning varies depending on the nature of the relationship. You love your spouse different than you love your sibling or your child. You love your dentist different than you love your favorite television show. Just as there are varied meanings to love, so are there varied ways of expressing it.

My friend's grandfather was a kind, but quiet man. I used to like going to his house when we were kids. One day my friend asked his grandmother, "How do you know Grandpa loves you? He never tells you so."

I never forgot his grandmother's response. She said, "He doesn't have to tell me, he shows me."

She proceeded to explain that her husband showed her he loved her every time he sacrificed his time to fill her car up with gas, wash the dishes, cut the grass, or do the million other selfless tasks that made her life easier.

Words are nice, but our actions will always speak louder—especially when it comes to love. With Valentine's Day approaching, now is a good time to consider how you show love to your teammates. Here are ten ways to do so:

1. **Bring them food.** Is there anything more appreciated than a timely snack? Providing food to a teammate who is ill or too busy to stop to get food demonstrates consideration and empathy.

2. **Show up on time.** Punctuality is a sign of respect, and respect is a sign of love. By showing up on time, you relieve your teammates of an unnecessary worry.

3. **Clean up after them when they are rushed.** Sometimes our teammates are pressed to meet deadlines and don't have enough time to tidy up after themselves before rushing out the door. Clean up their mess and give them one less thing to worry about when they return.

4. **Listen when they need to vent.** The previous points revolved around lightening your teammates' load, and in a way, so does this one. Pressure bursts pipes. By serving as a sounding board, you alleviate the pressure your teammates are feeling.

5. **Be present when they are lonely.** Sometimes people just need companionship. Striking up a conversation with someone who is feeling down can heal their

soul. It doesn't have to be a deep, probing conversation, either. The lighthearted ones are often the most meaningful.

6. **Defend them when others gossip behind their backs.** Loyalty is love and having the courage to stand up for someone when they aren't present to stand up for themselves is definitive loyalty.

7. **Celebrate their victories by bragging about them.** Rejoice in your teammates' success. Let others know how proud you are of what your teammates accomplished. The depth of your love is proportional to the outward expression of your joy.

8. **Ask them their opinions/Solicit their advice.** Asking a teammate what they think about an issue makes them feel valued. Remember to be an active listener when they're speaking, otherwise your inquiry will seem phony.

9. **Let something go that you might otherwise argue about.** Good teammates walk a fine line between holding others accountable and remaining above the fray. Occasionally, put the relationship ahead of the disagreement by overlooking minor issues. Silently, agree to disagree.

10. **Take a photo with them.** With the prominence of selfies on social media, sharing the photo spotlight with a teammate shows you are proud to be seen

with them. You let them—and others—know you wanted that moment to be forever captured.

Teams built on love have the greatest chance of experiencing sustained success. Why not choose to use this Valentine's Day as an occasion to let your teammates know how much you love them?

As always...Good teammates care. Good teammates share. Good teammates listen. Go be a good teammate.

Icarus Teammates
FEBRUARY 15

In Greek mythology, the story of Icarus is often used to warn of the perils of hubris (excessive confidence). Icarus was the adolescent son of Daedalus, a skilled artisan whom King Minos of Crete hired to build the Labyrinth that protected the palace from the menacing half bull, half man Minotaur.

After falling in disfavor with Minos, Daedalus and Icarus are imprisoned on the island. Daedalus devises a clever plan to escape Crete by fashioning wings for himself and his son from feathers they had gathered.

Before taking flight, however, Daedalus warns Icarus not to fly too close to the sun nor too close to the sea, lest the heat of the sun would melt the wax holding the feathers together and the spray of the sea would weigh them down.

Icarus initially heeds his father's advice, but soon becomes enamored by his newfound prowess. He soars higher and higher until his wings are eventually scorched by the sun, causing him to tumble from the sky and drown in the sea below.

The ancient Greeks considered hubris to be among the most dangerous character flaws. Hubris typically triggered the wrath of the gods and led to tragedy because it was viewed as an arrogant attempt to overstep mortal limitations.

Icarus teammates—team members with excessive, reckless confidence—can trigger similar wrath on their teams.

Icarus teammates don't consider the effect the risks they take have on the rest of their team. They are cavalier with their decisions, giving little forethought to the possibility of collateral damage. Much like their namesake, they overlook the consequences of flying too close to the proverbial sun.

In the business world, modern day examples of the damage caused by Icarus teammates can found in the tragic stories like Enron, Adelphia, and WorldCom. In the sports world, examples are found in recruiting violations, doping scandals, and point shaving.

Confidence is a necessary component of team success, as is the acceptance of inherent risk. Progress requires risk. To borrow a baseball analogy, you can't steal second with your foot on first.

So how can a team member exhibit the confidence to take risks without becoming an Icarus teammate? You avoid hubris by doing the following:

- Educate yourself on the potential consequences of your actions, especially the negative ones. Don't act impulsively, carelessly, or cluelessly.

- Consider how your actions will impact the entire team and not just you individually—*before* you act. An ounce of consideration can save a pound of regret.

- Seek the advice of someone wiser, more experienced, and capable of being emotionally objective about the situation. Had Icarus listened to Daedalus, his story would not have ended in tragedy.

By committing to being thorough, properly prepared, and only engaging in calculated risks, you limit the probability of being an Icarus teammate and increase the potential of being a good teammate.

As always…Good teammates care. Good teammates share. Good teammates listen. Go be a good teammate.

44

The Miracle of Nice
FEBRUARY 22

Do you believe in miracles? On this date in history, legendary sportscaster Al Michaels posed that iconic question to viewers during the final moments of the 1980 United States Olympic hockey team's upset of the Soviet Union.

The story of the match that came to be known as the "Miracle on Ice" was immortalized in the aptly titled 2004 Disney movie *Miracle*. In one of the movie's most memorable scenes, Coach Herb Brooks, portrayed by Kurt Russell, delivers a pregame speech capable of making even a stoic heart palpitate. Before his team's semi-final match against the heavily favored Soviets, Brooks gathers his players in the locker room. He stands silently in front of them, assessing their readiness. Then, he begins:

> *"Great moments are born from great opportunity. And that's what you have here tonight, boys. That's what you've earned here, tonight."*

As far as movies go, *Miracle* is considered to accurately depict true events, including dialogue. But did the real Herb Brooks speak those actual words in his pregame speech? It's hard to say.

There weren't any cameras rolling in the locker room that day. The speech Kurt Russell gives in the movie came from Jack O'Callahan, a player on the 1980 team who consulted on the script. Director Gavin O'Conner asked O'Callahan to write down as much of Brooks' speech as he could remember.

"I don't know if (Brooks) said, 'Great moments are made from great opportunities,' or if those are my words that sorta have taken on a life of their own," O'Callahan said in a 2015 interview with NPR radio.

"(The movie speech) wasn't word for word. There were some things in there that were probably what he said and some things that were just me putting my own words in there based on my memories. But when the guys all saw the movie, I actually asked a few guys, 'Is that kinda what he said before the game?' They were like, 'Yeah, pretty much.'"

No debate exists, however, about the accuracy of a shorter, far less eloquent speech Brooks gave two days later—one that did not make it into the movie.

After the "Miracle on Ice" match, the United States faced Finland in the finals. Losing to Finland would render their upset victory over the Soviets an otherwise unremarkable footnote.

Trailing Finland 2-1 after two periods, Brooks simply told his players during intermission: "If you lose this game, you'll take it to your (expletive) graves." He then turned and headed toward the door before pausing, looking back over his shoulder, and repeating, "Your (expletive) graves."

The coach left the locker room without saying another word. His team came out and scored three goals in the last period, en route to a 4-3 gold medal victory. The rest is, as they say, history.

Brooks' shorter, less eloquent, lesser-known finals "speech" offers an insightful glimpse into what haunts good teammates—regret.

Good teammates tie their worth to the extent of their service. Knowing that they could have done more to help their team causes them tremendous grief. The fear of regret motivates them to exhaust their efforts.

Hence, the miracle of good teammates' consistently being nice emanates from their commitment to eliminate regret from their lives.

So what "miracles" can you perform for your team today? Not sure? Start with being nice. The rest will miraculously take care of itself.

As always…Good teammates care. Good teammates share. Good teammates listen. Go be a good teammate.

The NPR interview referenced above is from Littlefield, Bill. "Hollywood Scores A 'Miracle' With Locker Room Speech." WBUR. June 6, 2015. https://www.wbur.org/onlyagame/2015/06/06/us-miracle-olympics-herb-brooks

45

Above the Clouds
MARCH 1

I was recently in Seattle, Washington for an event and got to visit nearby Mount St. Helens. I had never seen an active volcano before and thought renting a car for the short drive there would be worthwhile.

Fifty-seven people lost their lives when Mount St. Helens erupted on the morning of May 18, 1980, making it the deadliest explosion in U.S. history. The blast created a massive crater and reduced the mountain's height by more than a thousand feet.

Although none have matched the magnitude of the 1980 eruption, Mount St. Helens has had several smaller explosions since then and routinely experiences a variety of volcanic activity.

In full disclosure, I felt a little like Clark Griswald in the original *Vacation* movie when we pulled into the Mount St. Helens National Park Visitor's Center and were greeted by a sign that read: "Sorry, the Visitor's Center is closed until further notice."

We walked around the outside of the building, hoping to at least snag a photo of the volcano from their exterior observatory. Unfortunately, it was too foggy that morning to do so.

Disappointed with our luck, we started heading back to our car. That's when a park ranger emerged from the side of the building and asked us if we had any questions. Naturally, we did: "Is there any way for us to get a better view of Mount St. Helens?"

Ranger Adams chuckled and apologized for what she jokingly referred to as the abysmal "Pacific Northwet" weather. She asked us to wait while she went inside to check the "volcano cams."

A few minutes later, she returned to show us a clear image of Mount St. Helens on her phone. She told us that although the road to the highest viewpoint was closed due to snow, we could still get a great view of the peak if we drove far enough to get above the clouds.

Above the clouds? How far would we have to drive to do that? We were enveloped in dreariness, so I was skeptical of conditions being any better at higher elevations.

Ranger Adams sensed my apprehension but assured me that blue skies and clear views awaited us—above the clouds. She encouragingly said, "You came this far, you'll regret not trying to go farther."

Moved by her words, we headed off into the foggy unknown. We drove the windy, narrow road for almost thirty miles without any improvement in visibility. I was convinced we were on a goose hunt until out of nowhere the fog vanished.

Exactly as Ranger Adams had described, we were treated to sunshine, blue skies, and a clear view of Mount Saint Helens. The sight was truly majestic. The first thought that entered my mind: *Good teammate move*, Ranger Adams!

Sometimes we encounter occasions in our lives when we feel enveloped by abysmal conditions. Maybe it's a losing streak, a derailed career path, or a toxic relationship. It is during these occasions that we need a teammate like Ranger Adams who will encourage us to get above the clouds.

Once we rise beyond the fray of pettiness, jealousy, and selfishness, life becomes an entirely different experience. Our mood changes, apathy dissipates, and we discover clarity of purpose.

We all have it within us to encourage our teammates, but we also have it within us to be receptive to our teammates' encouragement with faithfulness. Having faith when the path to our desired "destination" is clouded by skepticism can be an equally impactful good teammate move.

I took a photo to include in my blog moments after we broke through the clouds. I will forever cherish this memory, as well as Ranger Adams' encouraging good teammate move.

Regrettably, I didn't think to take a photo of Ranger Adams as it would have made a nice accompaniment to this story. We stopped by the Visitor's Center to thank her on our way back down the mountain, but she was already gone.

If you happen to visit Mount Saint Helens in the near future and see Ranger Adams, be sure to convey my gratitude. As always…Good teammates care. Good teammates share. Good teammates listen. Go be a good teammate.

Five Impactful Things You Should Say to Your Teammates Every Day
MARCH 8

Consistency is the key to being a good teammate. What you consistently think, do, and say impacts your team's productivity and, ultimately, determines its level of success.

Research has shown that the words and phrases you *consistently* use when interacting with those whom you are closest—your teammates—influences how you are perceived and how you perceive the world around you.

Here are five impactful things good teammates should say to their fellow teammates every day:

1. **Good morning!** How enthusiastically you greet your teammates sets the tone for the rest of that day's interactions. To good teammates, "good" morning isn't only an extension of well wishes; it's a declaration of confidence. They are confidently

conveying their optimism that this morning will be a good morning.

2. **Can't wait to see you tomorrow!** How you greet your teammates is important, but so is how you leave them. Good teammates let their fellow teammates know they are looking forward to their next interaction. They leave others filled with eager anticipation for more.

3. **Nice job!** Good teammates make it a habit to recognize the commission of good teammate moves—kind, selfless acts that positively impact the team. They seek and seize opportunities to catch their teammates doing something right. And then they reward those actions with words (Nice job!, Way to go!, That's awesome!, etc.)

4. **Thank you!** If you can't find contributions that are worthy of your gratitude, you're not looking hard enough. Good teammates are genuinely grateful for even the smallest of their teammates' contributions. Appreciated contributions tend to evolve into repeated contributions. Small sacrifices, unselfish motives, and thoughtfulness deserve your appreciation.

5. **How can I help you?** This simple question may be the most impactful question you can ask a fellow teammate. Posing it conveys your willingness to

serve, an element of humility, and an interest in their problems. How you respond to their answer to this question can elevate your interest in their problem to your investment in their problem.

Consistency is the key to being a good teammate because consistency leads to trust. When others know what to expect from you, they start to trust you.

When your teammates trust that you are excited to see them, eager for their return, happy for their success, grateful for their contributions, and invested in their problems, you set your team up for success.

As always…Good teammates care. Good teammates share. Good teammates listen. Go be a good teammate.

The Value of Quality
MARCH 15

Are you familiar with the $5 haircut parable? Business schools often use it to illustrate effective counter-marketing tactics. I haven't required the services of a barbershop in quite some time, but even someone as follicly-challenged as me can appreciate the parable.

It goes something like this:

A barbershop had been an respected member of their local community for several generations. The family who ran the shop had a long-standing reputation for providing quality haircuts at a fair price.

One day, a national chain opens across the street and hangs a banner outside their salon advertising "$5 haircuts." The community was instantly attracted to the lower price.

As business boomed at the new salon, the family-owned barbershop fretted over what to do. Should they try to beat their competitor's price? They knew they couldn't sustain a lower price without putting themselves out of business.

They found themselves in a conundrum until the family patriarch came up with a solution.

He knew that quality differentiated their business from their competitor's, so he hung a banner outside their barbershop that simply stated: "We Fix $5 Haircuts."

The barbershop's business steadily returned once customers realized the value of quality—*quality* of product, *quality* of service, and *quality* of experience.

The "We fix $5 Haircuts" banner reminded the community that quality matters, especially when it comes to time and money. Sure, customers could save money with the quick $5 haircut, but their lack of satisfaction would eventually lead to wasted time and money.

Lately, I've been spending a lot of time working with talented teams who are failing to jell. I feel like a banner should hang outside my office that reads: "I Fix 5-Star Teams."

Too many leaders mistakenly think the quickest route to success is assembling a team with 5-Star talent—blue chip recruits with impressive resumes. In sports, these are persons with striking physical attributes who've acquired notable individual statistics. In business, they're graduates from the top schools who've acquired the best grades and highest test scores.

Talent plays a vital role in team success but only if that talent can work together. Hastily assembled 5-Star teams falter when their "talented" members are unable to sacrifice for the greater good, prioritize team needs ahead of individual agendas, or consider how their actions affect the rest of the team.

Much like the customers in the $5 haircut parable, team leaders need to consider the value of quality when evaluating an individual team member's worth. In this case, quality is found in that individual's capacity to be a good teammate.

Leaders who discount the value of good teammates eventually find themselves embroiled in pettiness, jealousy, and avoidable drama.

Leaders who place a premium on the value of good teammates eventually find themselves enveloped in camaraderie, harmony, and happiness.

As always…Good teammates care. Good teammates share. Good teammates listen. Go be a good teammate.

48

The Tanning Oil Incident
MARCH 22

Spring breakers have ascended on the Sunshine State! Resorts, beaches, and amusement parks are packed with northerners seeking reprieve from the cold. To Floridians, the expression "March Madness" isn't exclusive basketball.

My grandmother took my brother, cousin, and me on a spring break trip to Florida when I was in junior high. The trip was memorable for many reasons, not the least of which was me acquiring the worst sunburn of my life.

During our trip, we went to Wet 'n Wild—one of the largest water parks in the nation at that time. My grandmother dropped the three of us off at the gate with instruction to meet her back at the same spot when the park closed.

With sunglasses and towels in tow, we headed off for a day of fun. It didn't take long, however, for us to realize that we had made a regrettable mistake. We brought our sunglasses and towels but forgot our sunscreen.

The sun was starting to toast our pasty-white, northern skin. We found a kiosk in the park that sold sunscreen, but (as often is the case) the prices were outrageously high. Reluctantly, we spent some of the lunch money our grandmother had given us on the smallest, cheapest product they sold—something called "tanning oil."

Throughout the rest of the day, we lathered ourselves in tanning oil. Every time we took a break from the pool, we rubbed on another layer. Needless to say, we didn't tan; we burned.

When my grandmother returned to pick us up, she stared at us in disbelief. She knew instantly that the remainder of our trip wasn't going to be nearly as enjoyable.

I went to bed completely miserable that night. I woke up the next morning to find my skin a not-so-subtle shade of fire engine red, covered in sunburn blisters, and on the receiving end of my grandmother's *what-were-you-thinking* glare.

The lesson to be learned from my tanning oil incident is as much about ignorance, as it is the importance of warding off harmful UV rays.

We were old enough to know we needed protection from the sun, but not wise enough to know the difference between sunscreen and suntan oil. What we earnestly believed was preventing harm was making matters worse—and we were oblivious to our ignorance.

By the time we recognized our error, it was too late. The damage was already done.

Team members who are oblivious to their own ignorance are a hazard to a winning culture. It doesn't matter how noble or pure your intentions, if what you're doing is hurting the team, internal conflict will ensue.

Good teammates practice *intentional* self-awareness. By setting their pride aside, seeking the wisdom of others, and having the courage to discover their faults, they keep their ignorance from becoming willful ignorance.

Think about your habits and your interactions with your teammates. Is there anything you're doing that you assume is helping your team but may actually be hurting it? Choosing to learn that reality can keep your team from being burned.

As always...Good teammates care. Good teammates share. Good teammates listen. Go be a good teammate.

49

Breaking from the Brutal Truth
MARCH 29

In the category of cringeworthy moments, I rank hearing someone use the expression "brutally honest" near the top of the list. As in, "I'm going to be *brutally* honest" or "She was *brutally* honest" or "Can I be *brutally* honest?"

Whenever I hear someone preface their opinions with this absurdity, I immediately think: *Why does what you intend to say necessitate brutality?*

Brutality has no place in communication between caring team members. The nature of competition and complexities of team dynamics already include enough stress, it shouldn't be exacerbated by having to break the truth with brutality.

As Oliver Wendell Holmes said: "Don't flatter yourself that friendship authorizes you to say disagreeable things to your intimates. The nearer you come into relation with a person, the more necessary do tact and courtesy become."

Good teammates avoid brutality because they know it's little more than repackaged cruelty. People aren't generally receptive to, nor inspired by, cruelty. And they certainly aren't endeared by it.

Some would argue that the function of a good teammate is to be the bearer of difficult truths. Sure, occasions exist where team members are called to be guardians of the teams' culture. They must confront threatening behaviors by engaging in unpleasant conversations. But unpleasant conversations don't need to include unpleasant words. Consider the following sentences:

> Sentence A: *I think you're lazy.*
>
> Sentence B: *I believe you have it within you to work harder and do more.*

Both statements essentially have the same meaning. Both statements are presented as facts, or at least truthful opinions. Yet the brutality of the former stings more so than the latter. Sentence A is far more likely to cause a resentful, defensive, or dismissive response.

The purpose of caring communication is to ignite change, which is why good teammates choose to speak in a way that inspires without inflaming. They calculate their tone and timing.

Brutality is sometimes inflicted in the spirit of efficiency. The speaker purports to eliminate tact in favor of delivering a simpler, blunter message. They'll try to mask their forthcoming brutality by "cutting straight to the point."

What is delivered, however, usually leads to an inefficient outcome. The speaker inevitably ends up having to navigate hurt feelings, battle bitterness, and repair damaged relationships. Nothing about any of those outcomes is efficient.

Individuals who choose to speak the brutal truth choose to be ego crushers. They suppress their teammates' confidence through cruelty.

Good teammates don't crush egos; they caress them. They use their words to inspire change. By steering clear of brutality, good teammates empower you to see what you can become.

As always…Good teammates care. Good teammates share. Good teammates listen. Go be a good teammate.

Luis the Uber Driver
APRIL 5

Uber drivers are an interesting breed. They've become the source of some of my favorite stories. Over the past few months, I've met drivers who were refugees escaping war-torn countries, extras who appeared in blockbuster movies, Harvard students working their way through graduate school, and tech entrepreneurs building capital to finance their creations.

During my recent excursion to Los Angeles, I happened upon the most interesting of all Uber drivers—a driver with a perfect five-star rating.

I like to browse my Uber drivers' credentials while I'm waiting for them to arrive. I noticed that my approaching driver, Luis, held a five-star rating. I immediately assumed he was a new driver. Typically, new drivers are the only ones who show perfect ratings. But a click on Luis' profile photo revealed, to my surprise, that he had completed over 32,000 trips.

To have maintained a perfect rating through that many trips is no small feat. In fact, it's practically unheard of. Frivolous reports are common in ride sharing apps. Sometimes a passenger doesn't like how the car smells or thinks the seats are uncomfortable or doesn't like the driver's music. It's hard to please everybody all the time. The laws of probability—and pettiness—are not in an Uber driver's favor.

I could hardly wait for Luis to arrive to ask him about his perfect rating. The moment I opened the car door, I launched into him: "Luis, is it true that you've done 32,000 trips and still have a perfect rating?"

He smiled and said, "No."

I knew it! There was a mistake in the system. Nobody can maintain a five-star rating through that many trips. But before I could bring the error to Luis's attention, he said, "I have over 50,000 trips—32,000 with Uber and another 20,000 with Lyft. I do both apps and I have a perfect rating on both."

That clarification made me even more intrigued. I asked him how he achieved such a miraculous distinction, to which he replied: "Respect. I treat everybody with respect."

His reply lacked the depth I was hoping for, so I probed further. To Luis, respect was tied to happiness. Before he became a full-time Uber driver, he managed a variety of businesses, including an auto parts store and several restaurants.

In his previous line of work, he found it difficult to keep everyone happy. He had to keep his customers happy. He had to keep his staff happy. He had to keep his vendors happy.

And he had to keep his bosses happy. That was too many people to keep happy.

As an Uber driver, he only had to keep one entity happy—his passengers. This was a far easier task to accomplish. By showing respect, anticipating their needs, and empathizing with their problems, Luis kept his passengers happy. Happy passengers leave good reviews.

Team members can fall into the trap of trying to keep everyone on their team happy. But doing so will likely leave them as frustrated as Luis was with his previous jobs. Rarely does everyone on the team have the same needs or share the same perspectives.

The trick to being a good teammate is respecting everyone's unique perspectives without compromising the team's needs. In other words, choose to view the team as the "one entity" you strive to keep happy.

Sometimes keeping the team happy will translate into accommodating individual needs; sometimes it will mean sacrificing individual needs—including your own. Knowing that you chose what is best for the team over what is best for the individual affords you a sense of inner peace, which enables happiness.

When we arrived at my destination, I thanked Luis for his insights. In typical good teammate fashion, he respectfully declined my gratitude, saying, "No. Thank YOU for letting me be your driver." With those words, he earned yet another five-star rating.

As always...Good teammates care. Good teammates share. Good teammates listen. Go be a good teammate.

The Eyes Have It
APRIL 12

I was working with a group of corporate leaders who were engaged in a heated discussion about how they should handle a shady business practice of their top competitor.

One leader thought the appropriate response was to do to their competitor what their competitor was doing to them. He justified his line of thinking with the all too familiar "An eye for and eye…"

Another leader opposed that response, believing it to be unethical and beneath their company. He countered the first suggestion by quoting Mahatma Gandhi: "An eye for an eye will leave the whole world blind."

Sensing the escalating tension, a third leader quipped, "Well, I guess the eyes have it."

The exchange, including the third leader's witty interjection, caused me to think about how crucial our eyes are to being a good teammate. Good teammates look each other in the eyes when they speak. They listen with their ears

165

and their eyes. And they keep an eye out for struggling teammates.

Here are four other prominent "eye" quotes that apply to the art of being a good teammate:

1. **"Beauty lies in the eye of the beholder."** Though often credited to poet Oscar Wilde (1890), variations of this expression about interpreting beauty can also found in Shakespeare's *Love Labours Lost* (1588) and Ben Franklin's *Poor Richard's Almanack* (1741). Good teammates aren't charmed by the superficial. They appreciate other perspectives and respect the idea that an individual's true beauty stems from what's on the inside. Good teammates judge people by the size of their heart (i.e., their being in *The WE Gear*), not the clothes they wear, the color of their skin, or any other inconsequential markers.

2. **"The eyes are the windows to your soul."** The origins of this quote are somewhat of a mystery, as well. Shakespeare, Da Vinci, and Cicero have all been cited as being the original orator. Regardless of who should get credit, the quote holds tremendous truth about a good teammate's authenticity. When you peer into a good teammate's eyes, you see sincerity. The purity of their intentions is evident. You immediately know they have no hidden agendas or ulterior motives. They are committed to doing whatever is best for their team.

3. **"I can't shave with my eyes closed."** No debate surrounds who said this quote. Carl Winslow, the fictional policeman portrayed by Reginald VelJohnson on the sitcom *Family Matters*, said it in the tenth episode when explaining why he refused to take a bribe. Good teammates do not compromise their integrity. They're able to look at the person staring back at them in the mirror without shame or regret.

4. **"Keep your eyes on the stars, and your feet on the ground."** Theodore Roosevelt delivered these words in an early twentieth century speech prior to becoming president of the United States. The speech's purpose was to remind people to remain humble and be practical. Good teammates are goal-driven. They have a growth mindset. But they are also ego-less. They don't allow success to go to their head or prevent them from serving the needs of their teams.

If none of the above "eye" quotes happen to resonate with you, consider that when it comes to good teammates, the eyes do indeed have it. Good teammates have the *eye of the tiger*, they're the *apple of their leader's eye*, they *keep their eye on the prize,* they don't turn a *blind eye* to bad behaviors, and their addition can change a team's culture in the *blink of an eye.*

As always…Good teammates care. Good teammates share. Good teammates listen. Go be a good teammate.

Confining Moments
APRIL 19

When I was in fourth grade, a classmate tripped and broke his arm while we were playing tag football on the playground. The teacher monitoring recess thought his trip was the result of us being too rough, so she ended recess early and sent us all back to our classroom.

We were supposed to sit quietly at our desks and reflect on what we had done until our homeroom teacher, Mr. Morris (named changed to protect his identity), arrived. But fourth graders being fourth graders made her instructions unlikely to be observed.

Some of my classmates started getting out of their seats. Others began chatting with their neighbors. It wasn't long before soft chatter and quiet visits turned into full-blown rambunctiousness.

Mr. Morris stormed into the room and immediately tore into our class. He scolded us for not following instructions.

He scolded us for being too loud. And he scolded us for having foolish priorities.

He emphasized the last point by stating that he didn't know why we were wasting our time playing football because none of us were ever going to play professionally or even earn a scholarship to play in college.

For reasons I cannot explain, one of my classmates mustered the nerve to respond to Mr. Morris' dreadful declaration: "What about Donny? He's always the best player at recess no matter whose team he is on."

"Donny?" Mr. Morris exclaimed in disbelief. "Donny can't even pass fourth grade. He's not going to make a living playing football."

Donny was a quiet kid. He usually just sat it the back of the room and kept to himself. I don't suspect Donny had a great home life, as he seemed to wear the same soiled clothes to school every day. His hair was often shaggy and unkempt, and he never had money for book fairs, extra cafeteria snacks, or anything else of that nature.

Despite all of Donny's deficiencies, he was a marvel on the playground football field. He could throw and kick the ball farther than any other boy in our class and he rarely dropped a pass that was thrown to him.

Mr. Morris was right in that Donny struggled in school. Donny had flunked fourth grade the previous year and was forced to repeat the grade. His being a year older than the rest of us surely contributed to his athletic prowess, but it didn't excuse Mr. Morris' cruelty.

I remember Donny perking up in his seat and smiling when our classmate refuted Mr. Morris' assertion. (*What about Donny?*) In hindsight, I doubt any peer had ever so openly professed such high praise for Donny prior to that moment.

But as quickly as that praise had invigorated Donny, Mr. Morris' response deflated him. (*Donny can't even pass fourth grade.*) Donny dropped his head and sank into the confines of his crushed spirit.

I don't know whatever became of Donny, other than he didn't become a professional football player. To the best of my recollection, he never even tried out for our high school's varsity football team. I haven't thought about Donny or that moment in Mr. Morris' fourth grade class in a long time.

A few weeks ago, the sports world celebrated the anniversary of the 1982 NCAA Basketball Championship game between the University of North Carolina and Georgetown University. Many know this game because of the late-game heroics of a then relatively unknown Tar Heel freshman named Michael Jordan.

With his team trailing 62-61, Jordan hit a jump shot with seventeen seconds left on the clock that turned out to be the game winning basket. For all intents and purposes, that shot launched the megastar's career and became a defining moment in his life.

However, basketball purists know that Jordan's shot wasn't actually the deciding play of the 1982 championship game. After Jordan scored, Georgetown got the ball back with enough time to regain their lead.

Georgetown guard Fred Brown dribbled up the court and began to set the Hoya's offense. But in the confusion of the transition, Brown errantly passed the ball to North Carolina's James Worthy, mistaking Worthy for Georgetown teammate Eric Smith.

Brown's pass is viewed as one of sports' all-time biggest gaffes. It became a defining moment of Brown's life. Yet Georgetown coach John Thompson's response kept the play from becoming a confining moment of Brown's life.

When the game ended, Thompson embraced an emotional, dejected Brown. "Don't worry about it," Thompson whispered in Brown's ear. "You've won a lot more games for me than you've lost."

I ultimately decided against writing about Michael Jordan, Fred Brown, and the 1982 NCAA title game. Plenty has already been written about that game by better writers than me. But learning about Coach Thompson's response to Fred Brown caused me to think about the interaction between Mr. Morris and Donny, and I've continued to think about it ever since.

Good teammates don't allow defining moments to become confining moments. Mr. Morris' choice in words turned what could have been Donny's defining moment into a confining moment.

What if instead of "Donny can't even pass fourth grade," Mr. Morris had said "Well, if Donny buckles down and improves his grades, he's got a chance to earn a football scholarship and play in the pros."

Had Mr. Morris responded differently, he could have injected the sort of inspiration into Donny's spirit that changes a life's trajectory. He could have freed Donny from the confines of past failures.

You may have noticed that I paraphrased most of the above story, except for what Mr. Morris said about Donny. I used quotation marks for that part because, decades later, I can still remember his exact words with vivid clarity.

What transpired with Mr. Morris wasn't only a confining moment for Donny, it was confining moment for everyone in that class, including me. I didn't agree with what Mr. Morris said. I regret not having the courage to immediately get out of my seat, walk straight over to Donny, and insist that he not be discouraged by Mr. Morris' opinion. Because that's all it was—one man's opinion.

Mr. Morris retired from teaching some years ago. Judging the totality of his career based on that single interaction would be unfair. Maybe he was having a bad day. Maybe he let his anger get the best of him. Maybe he regrets what he said. Maybe he doesn't even remember the incident.

The story of Mr. Morris is worth sharing though, because it can prevent another Mr. Morris from confining the next Donny. Prevention begins with awareness, and what better to be aware of than the missteps of those who traveled the path before us.

When good teammates come to clutch moments, they take a beat. They pause to consider the impact of what they are about to say. In the *confines* of that moment, good teammates turn confining moments back into defining moments by choosing words that will empower the recipient.

As always…Good teammates care. Good teammates share. Good teammates listen. Go be a good teammate.

Bring the Good Teammate
Message to Your Team

Are you interested in bringing the "Good Teammate" message to your event or implementing strategies to improve the quality of the teammates you have on your team? If so, contact Lance Loya at:

Phone: (814) 659-9605

E-mail: info@coachloya.com

Website: www.coachloya.com

Twitter: @coachlanceloya

Facebook: facebook.com/coachloya

Instagram: @coachlanceloya

LinkedIn: linkedin.com/in/coachloya

Join the movement and sign up for Lance Loya's weekly *Teammate Tuesday* blog at *www.coachloya.com/blog.*

*If you have enjoyed this book or it has inspired you in some way, we would love to hear from you! Be a good teammate and share your photos and stories with us through email or social media. We want to hear from you!

About the Author

Lance Loya is the founder and CEO of The Good Teammate Factory. As a leading authority on team dynamics, he specializes in getting individuals to shift their focus from *me* to *we*. Other experts concentrate on improving teamwork, but Lance concentrates on improving the teammate. Lance's method works!

Lance has authored nine books on the subject of being a good teammate, including *The WE Gear*, which made *Forbes'* list of "20 Books to Make You a Better Coach or Mentor."

A college basketball coach turned author, blogger, podcaster, and professional speaker, he is known for his enthusiastic personality and his passion for turning *teambusters* into good teammates. Lance has inspired readers and audiences around the globe through his books, keynotes, and seminars.

When not speaking or writing, he is a loyal husband to his high school sweetheart and a doting father to his two daughters—who, incidentally, were the impetus behind his heartwarming children's book.

Also by Lance Loya

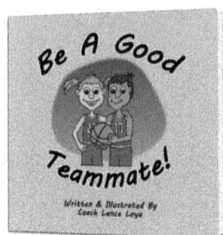

Be a Good Teammate

An illustrated children's book teaches the importance of teamwork and how to be a good teammate. Good teammates care, share, and listen. You don't have to play sports to be on a team. This book encourages kindness and counters bullying.

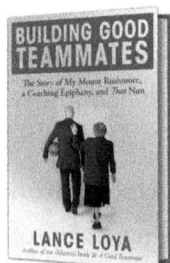

Building Good Teammates

The story of Lance Loya's discovery of an alternative approach to coaching players to be good teammates explores how his personal Mount Rushmore—the four men who had the biggest impact on his life—and a quirky nun influenced his coaching methodology.

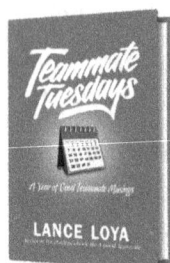

Teammate Tuesdays

In this compilation of the entire first year of Lance Loya's popular weekly blog of the same name, each chapter examines a different aspect of being a good teammate. Gain insight and encouragement through a variety of "good teammate" observations.

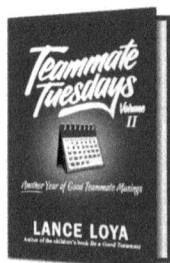

Teammate Tuesdays Vol. II

Go deeper into the world of good teammates in this compilation of another entire year of Lance Loya's popular weekly blog of the same name. Includes *musings* ranging from touching stories to creative ideas for inspiring team members to become better teammates.

Also by Lance Loya

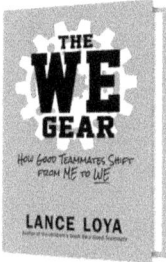

The WE Gear

Discover how good teammates shift from *me* to *WE*. Everybody wants teamwork on their team, but teamwork does not happen without good teammates—individuals whose unique way of thinking propels their team to success no matter what team they are on.

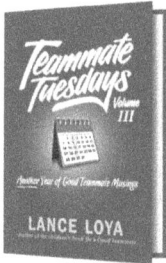

Teammate Tuesdays Vol. III

In this third installment of the *Teammate Tuesdays* series, Lance Loya once again chronicles a year of his journey exploring what it means to be a good teammate. Fifty-two weeks of observations unfold through fifty-two short, easily digestible chapters.

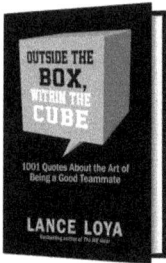

Outside the Box, Within the Cube

Be inspired by this collection of 1,001 quotes about the art of being a good teammate. Quotes motivate us to become better versions of ourselves. They lift us up when we feel down, guide us when we feel lost, and empower us when we feel constrained.

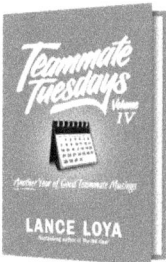

Teammate Tuesdays Vol. IV

The fourth edition of the *Teammate Tuesdays* series continues to probe the art of being a good teammate. Like the previous volumes, each of the book's fifty-two chapters addresses a different element of teamwork and the concept of being a good teammate.

Celebrate Your Teammates

Good teammates make being part of the team worthwhile! That's why on July 22, **National Be a Good Teammate Day** recognizes the sacrifices, kindness, and generosity of these selfless individuals.

Whether it's sports, family, community, school, or work, everybody is part of a team. Use the day to show your appreciation to those willing to put the needs of their "team" ahead of themselves.

Honor their contributions to the team with a boisterous "Thank you!" or a well-deserved high five or hug. Be sure to let the world know how grateful you are by sharing a photo of you and a good teammate on social media, using the hashtag:

#NationalBeAGoodTeammateDay

Listen to the Podcast

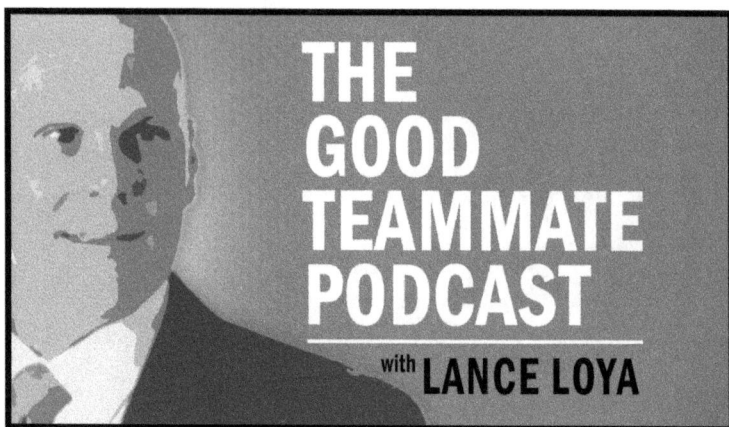

Do you like to listen to podcasts during your daily commute or while you work out? Check out The Good Teammate Podcast! Listening to Lance Loya discuss the art of being a good teammate through short audio selections from his *Teammate Tuesday* blog is guaranteed to inject a dose of happiness into your life.

The Be a Good Teammate Podcast is available on Apple Podcasts, Google Podcasts, Amazon Music, Spotify, TuneIn Radio, and Anchor.

You can download past episodes or subscribe to receive notifications about the release of new episodes. To learn more, visit:

www.coachloya.com/podcast/

Learn from a Course

The Good Teammate Factory offers online video courses to help teams gain greater insight in the art of being a good teammate. Courses are available for both sports and corporate teams and are an ideal way to improve teamwork, reduce selfishness, and draw teams closer together.

Teams engage in the course content and activities together in a group setting such as a meeting room or classroom. The courses are flexible in that they can be completed in a single sitting or divided up and stretched out over a series of meetings.

If you want to improve teamwork, send your team to The Good Teammate Factory!

WWW.GOODTEAMMATEFACT☼RY.COM

Take the Quiz

The Good Teammate Quiz

Are *you* a good teammate? Your team's potential for achieving success is ultimately dependent upon your answer to this question. Everybody wants teamwork on their team, but teamwork doesn't happen without good teammates—individuals who prioritize team objectives over personal agendas.

Gaining insight into the kind of a teammate you are increases your awareness for how your actions impact the other members of your team. It also increases the likelihood of your team working together to achieve genuine synergy.

Take the good teammate quiz today to assess your aptitude for practicing good teammate behaviors! To learn more about the quiz, visit:

www.coachloya.com/quiz/